THE ENCYCLOPEDIA OF ORIGAMI & PAPERCRAFT

PAUL JACKSON

D0928269

HEADLINE

A QUARTO BOOK

Copyright © 1991 Quarto Publishing plc

First published in Great Britain in 1991 by
HEADLINE BOOK PUBLISHING PLC

First published in paperback in 1992
by HEADLINE BOOK PUBLISHING PLC

All rights reserved. No part of this publication may be reproduced, stored
in a retrieval system, or transmitted, in any form or by any means without
the prior permission in writing of the publisher, nor be otherwise
circulated in any form of binding or cover other than that in which it is
published and without a similar condition including this condition being
imposed on the subsequent purchaser.

British Library Cataloguing in Publication Data
Jackson, Paul
  The Encyclopedia of origami and papercraft techniques.
  1. Handicrafts using paper
  745.54

ISBN 0-7472-7888-1

This book was designed and produced by
Quarto Publishing plc
The Old Brewery
6 Blundell Street
London N7 9BH

Senior editor Kate Kirby
Editor Mary Senechal
Designer Richard Mellor
Photographers Ian Howes, David Birch
Art director Moira Clinch
Publishing director Janet Slingsby

With thanks to Mellor Design Ltd, David Kemp, Paul Forrester,
Stefanie Foster

Typeset by En to En, Tunbridge Wells
Manufactured in Singapore by Chroma Graphics Pte Ltd.
Printed by Star Standard Industries (Pte) Ltd

The paperworks shown in this book are the copyright of the individual
artists, and may not be reproduced for commercial purposes.

HEADLINE BOOK PUBLISHING PLC
Headline House
79 Great Titchfield Street
London W1P 7FN

CONTENTS

FOREWORD

Paper is the most versatile of all art and craft materials. The breadth of techniques – from the "dry" paper arts, such as origami, pop-ups and paper sculpture, to the "wet" arts, such as papermaking and papier mâché – is unequalled. Paper is also quick and easy to work, inexpensive, and needs only the minimum of basic equipment. Much can be achieved with relatively little experience.

And yet paper is only now achieving respect in the West as a creative medium. The reasons are diverse: a deeper awareness of Oriental culture and its esteem for the paper arts; the commercial success of pop-up books and greeting cards; the growth and consolidation of creative origami; the rise of interest in many traditional crafts, including papermaking; and the patronage given to contemporary paper artists by galleries and collectors. Perhaps the new-found respect for a material as humble and tactile as paper is an intuitive reaction against an increasingly technological world. Or it could simply be paper's turn to be fashionable. Whatever the reason, a material once merely functional has now become cultural too.

This book is a timely response to the growing interest in paper. The first section – TECHNIQUES – provides a step-by-step guide to the fundamental techniques of the major paper arts; the second section THEMES presents a gallery of outstanding paperworks.

If you wish to create your own paperworks but are unsure how to begin, start with the exercises and projects relating to a particular technique, then experiment playfully to develop a personal style, perhaps with an abstract or representational theme in mind to guide you. If you are searching for a theme, refer to the paperworks in the THEMES section for ideas.

I hope this book will inspire you to create with paper, and that you will come to know the many pleasures of working with this extraordinary material.

Paul Jackson

PART ONE
TECHNIQUES

A sound knowledge of technique lies behind any creative achievement. This part of the book aims to help you develop your creativity by explaining the fundamental techniques of the major papercrafts. It will, of course, be a matter of temperament whether you work your way carefully through the explanatory exercises and projects or just use them as a basis for creating your own paperworks, but practising the procedures that underlie all papercrafts will increase the knowledge and skill that open the way to creativity. Once the guidelines are in place, you are free to break away from them to express your own original ideas in paper.

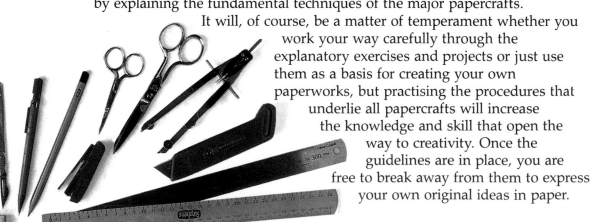

There is a stimulating variety of papercrafts and where they do share techniques, such as folding, cutting and bending, these are generally applied in different ways. Nevertheless, the technical approach to all the dry crafts, such as origami and pop-ups, is broadly similar, as is the approach to the wet crafts of papier mâché and papermaking. The dry crafts use techniques that are mostly measured, geometric and precise. Wet crafts are more spontaneous, more decorative and less engineering-based. The two categories are complementary, each appealing to particular qualities and answering particular creative requirements.

The techniques described here provide a solid foundation from which creative work in dry or wet papercrafts can develop, and with interest in these crafts growing, those who would like to pursue their knowledge of a specific craft still further may well be able to do so through a local evening class or an art college course.

A knowledge of techniques alone, however, will not create memorable paperworks. That more enigmatic quality of imagination must operate alongside the understanding of technique, each stimulating the other. The results of such interaction can be seen in the THEMES section of the book, where paper artists have put the techniques described on the following pages to use.

ALL ABOUT PAPER

ALL ABOUT GRAIN

CREASING PAPER

Although it is a common material, sources for the supply of paper may not be immediately apparent. However, with only a little research, a pleasing variety of papers and cards can be found, some of which may inspire paperworks that would not otherwise have been made. The three sources suggested here should all be useful.

Art and craft shops

All cities – and towns of any size – have these shops, most of which stock a reasonably good selection of papers. Some major cities have shops which specialize in selling papers and these are worth a visit.

Local printers

All printers keep stocks of papers and cards bought in for specific printing jobs, and because they buy in bulk, some sheets invariably remain unused. Prices per sheet will be considerably lower than shop prices, but you will probably have to buy a minimum quantity.

Paper merchants

Paper merchants do not make paper, but buy it direct from paper mills or from paper manufacturers to sell on to printers and other users.

Nearly all will supply swatches of papers (small sample books) free of charge. Many will deliver large sample sheets without charge or for a nominal sum, though further sheets will be at the regular price. If you are able to give a company address for delivery rather than a private one, you may well be able to order a large number of sample sheets without charge. Merchants also frequently sell packs containing all the colours and weights of a particular range of paper, at cost. These are a bargain. To find a merchant, look under "Paper merchant" in the business section of a telephone directory.

Types of paper

Papers and cards are usually developed and manufactured to be used by the packaging industry and commercial or fine art printers. Consequently, a bewildering number of papers are available for particular uses, each with its own set of complex technical specifications. These specifications need not necessarily concern the paper artist to whom the look and feel of a paper is more important. There are, however, a few basic paper types and terms which may prove useful.

Acid free paper

Paper from which all acids have been removed during manufacturing in order to improve its strength and colour. It should have a pH number of 7.07 or higher and should not yellow or become brittle quickly. Wood pulp – the basic component of most paper – is naturally acidic, which is why low-quality, chemically untreated newsprint, used for newspapers and some paperback books, deteriorates rapidly.

Bond paper

Paper which has been "sized" (sealed with a gluey mixture) to prevent penetration by writing or drawing inks. Stationery papers are commonly described as bond papers. Printing papers are lightly sized and are not usually referred to as bond.

Coated paper

Papers coated with an additional surface to give a smoother finish and therefore greatly improve printing quality. A coating of a different colour from the bulk of the paper may crack when creased to reveal an unsightly white line, so colour-coated papers should not be scored.

Laid paper

Paper with a pattern of fine parallel lines, appearing either as ridges and furrows or as opaque and translucent bands.

Rag paper

Paper containing a high percentage of fibre from cotton or linen fabrics, including recycled clothing. A rag paper is usually of very high quality and will fade or yellow only with great age. Rag papers are commonly used by artists for watercolours and etching.

Wove paper

Paper with a very faint mesh pattern, rather than the parallel lines of laid paper.

Paper weights

Weight is a guide to a paper's other properties and to its price. In Britain, Europe and most countries except the United States, weight is expressed in terms of the weight in grams of a sheet of paper one metre square. Thus, photocopy paper is said to be 80gsm (or $80gm^2$), because a sheet 1m $\times$ 1m weighs 80 grams. Thinner paper, such as airmail paper, is approximately 45gsm, and thicker paper, such as cartridge (drawing paper), is about 150gsm.

Above 250gsm, paper officially becomes card. Above 500gsm, weights are usually abandoned and cards are identified by thickness, measured in microns.

Some papers and cards are unusually compacted or aerated, so they appear to have a high or low grammage compared to thickness. Therefore, thickness is not necessarily a reliable indicator of weight.

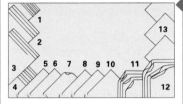

Key to papers

1 Paper merchant coloured paper.
2 Paper merchant added fibre effect.
3 Paper merchant marble effect.
4 Paper merchant different "coloured" parchment effect.
5 Acid free.
6 Bonded.
7 Coated.
8 Laid.
9 Rag.
10 Wove.
11 Coloured one side.
12 Coloured both sides.
13 Decorative origami paper.

Almost all construction work with paper and card must take account of the grain in the sheet. For ease of reference, therefore, and because this matter is so central to all papercrafts (with the possible exceptions of PAPIER MÂCHÉ, PULPING and PAPERMAKING) the use of grain is discussed here rather than being repeated within individual sections. Much of the remainder of the book assumes some knowledge of these matters, so if they are unfamiliar to you, please spend a little time on this section.

All machine-made papers and cards have a grain, formed as the glutinous hair-like fibres that stick together to form the sheet are vibrated to lie in line with the direction of travel of the moving belt that pulls the pulp from the "wet" end of manufacture to the "dry", gradually creating the paper. Handmade papers do not have a grain, as the fibres lie randomly about the sheet.

When drawing or painting on paper, the grain is of little relevance. However, when paper is folded, rolled, torn or cut, the influence of the fibres lying in parallel can be critical.

Testing for the grain

1 To find the direction of the grain, bend a sheet in half several times (do not crease it) to gauge the spring.

2 Then, turn the sheet through 90 degrees and bring the other two edges together. A difference in tensions will be apparent. The sheet will bend more easily along the line of the fibres, or "with the grain". It will not be as flexible when bent across the line of the fibres, or "against the grain". If you have never noticed it before, this is a very surprising phenomenon!

Creasing with the grain

The tendency of a sheet to fold more easily when creased with the grain becomes ever more apparent the heavier and thicker the paper used. A crease made against the grain on a sheet of heavy paper or card will often produce a rough, broken edge at the fold.

So, whenever possible, crease heavier sheets with the grain, not against it. This would apply, for example, to the construction of INCISED POP-UPS, where all the creases are parallel.

A crease at an angle to the grain – particularly if it is one of only a few creases on the sheet – will produce unequal tensions to either side and distort the surface of the sheet. Therefore, a shape cut out from a larger sheet may have to be oriented so that any creases on the cut-out lie parallel to the grain, not at an angle to it.

▲ Here, the top sheet has been creased against the grain to create a rough edge, whereas the bottom sheet has been creased with the grain, to create a smoother edge.

Tearing

As could be predicted, a sheet will tear more cleanly with the grain than against it.

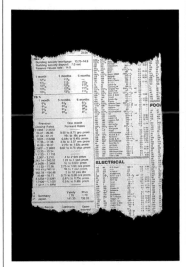

▲ To test this, tear a sheet of newspaper first downwards, then across. The difference is pronounced.

Rolling

◄ When rolling cylinders, the paper will roll more readily with the grain, so that tighter cylinders can be formed.

Always carry large sheets of paper or card rolled into a loose tube along the line of the grain. This may sometimes mean rolling one long edge to the opposite one to create a longer tube than may seem necessary, but the paper will be less stressed. Rolling against the grain can leave disfiguring buckle marks on the sheet. When buying paper in a shop, always insist that heavier weights are rolled the correct way, with the grain.

Pleated form

The sheet has been pre-creased and collapsed without cuts to create a form with a remarkable load-bearing capability, but which is also very flexible. It is hand-creased from lightweight paper. The crease pattern is so complex that the direction of the grain has no influence on its construction.

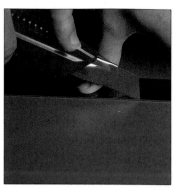

Creasing by hand
Before deciding to crease by hand, crease a small piece of the sheet both with and against the grain. If the folded edges are clean and unbroken, the sheet can be creased by hand. If the folded edges are broken, the paper is too heavy to crease by hand and should be scored, cut-scored or indented (see right).

The majority of papermaking techniques involves making creases. As with GRAIN (see previous two pages) the basics of creasing are discussed here, rather than being repeated within individual sections.

Creasing is so elementary that it is frequently done without regard for the best method. One of the following four methods will be ideal for any crease on any sheet. Choice depends on the weight of the sheet and the use to which the crease is being put.

1 Rest the paper on a smooth, hard, level surface. Orientate the paper so that the line of the crease about to be made runs horizontally from left to right across your body. Pick up the edge or corner nearest to you.

2 Take the edge or corner to whatever position is necessary to locate the line of the crease, then make the crease. Always ensure that the crease is made at the bottom of the sheet, never down the side or across the top.

Not all creases should be made against a surface. Smaller creases, particularly in ORIGAMI, are best made with the paper in the air.

Scoring
This is an easy way to crease heavy paper and card, but has the disadvantage of weakening the sheet at the folded edge, because the surface of the sheet has been cut.

1 Place a straight edge along the line of the crease and score with a sharp craft knife, cutting two-thirds of the way through the card. Always score on the outer, or mountain, side of a crease. Some practice may be necessary to cut to the correct depth.

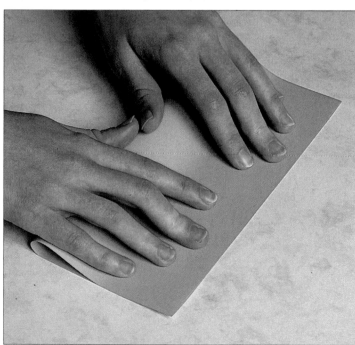

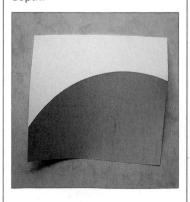

2 Scoring is ideal for constructing curved creases, which can be made freehand. This technique is much used in PAPER SCULPTURE.

Cut-score

A technique midway between scoring and indenting, cut-scoring should be used either for creasing very thick card or for giving thinner card a particularly flexible crease, such as might be needed on a box lid.

Indenting

This is the technique used to crease commercially manufactured cartons and boxes. The card is not weakened by scoring, but is indented under pressure along the line of the crease. This is achieved by stamping the card with a metal edge similar to the edge of a metal rule. The same result can be achieved by hand.

► Use thick, strong card. Cut it into two parts, each with at least one perfectly straight edge. Tape each part to a flat backing surface, so that the straight edges are 3mm ($^1/_{10}$in) apart. Lay the card to be creased over the gully between the two parts, so that the line of the crease about to be made

exactly follows the line of the gully. Push the card into the gully with a blunt scissor point, forming the crease.

▲ The card is cut all the way through in a series of dashes formed by a craft knife held against a rule. The length of the cuts and the distance between them depends on the thickness of the card and the degree of flexibility required, though clearly the longer the cuts, the weaker will be the card. Indent the crease for added flexibility (see right).

PAUL JACKSON
Folded form
► This simple but surprisingly stable form is one of a long series of "one crease" studies, in which the author explored the possibilities of single creases put into a square sheet of paper. The crease here is made by hand in a lightweight paper, but could have been made using any of the techniques on this spread, provided a paper or card of the appropriate weight was used. Height: 15cm (6in)

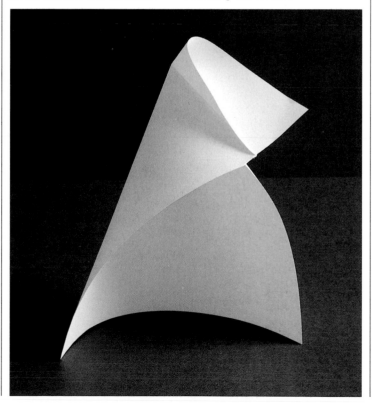

ORIGAMI

Origami is the best known of all papercrafts, perhaps because it is the easiest to define and because most of us have done a little of it as children. Its strict rules permit no cutting, no gluing and no decoration of the paper: the sheet may only be folded. Rules are there to be broken, and many non-origami paper artists also use basic folding techniques in their work.

The origins and history of the art are obscure. The word itself is Japanese: *ori,* to fold and *kami,* paper (becoming *gami* when combined with *ori*). The name is a tribute to the ancestral home of the art, though it is a matter of dispute whether the Japanese, Koreans or Chinese were the first to fold paper as a creative art. The Japanese developed sophisticated origami forms some 1,200 years ago, usually for symbolic or ceremonial purposes, and, contrary to subsequent rules, these were frequently cut. With the coming of Western influences in the late nineteenth century, indigenous symbolism largely disappeared. Origami became recreational and of little consequence.

In the 1930s a young Japanese man, Akira Yoshizawa, began developing new forms from the surviving traditional ones. His single-minded dedication and creative genius helped establish origami as a creative art form.

Paper folding in the West, with the exception of a minor creative period in Spain early in the twentieth century, remained largely a schoolchild's diversion. However, in the early 1950s, a renowned British-based stage illusionist, Robert Harbin, became fascinated by the creative potential of paper folding. He collected as many traditional designs as he could (a surprising number), invented some of his own, and in 1956 published *Paper Magic.* The book established the creative potential of the art in the West. Subsequent books by Harbin and the US paper folder Sam Randlett consolidated its position and introduced the word "origami".

Since that time, in the Oriental and the Western world, tens of thousands of designs have been created in a remarkable range of styles. Origami has an appeal possibly broader than that of any other papercraft. For many it is a form of puzzle-solving, attempting to make a model from diagrams in a book with the satisfaction of having an impressive object at the

conclusion. For others it is a branch of mathematics or an entertaining party trick, a vocabulary for design, or perhaps an educational aid. It is art, science and play: recreational yet essentially profound.

Materials

There are no strictures regarding choice of paper. Many people like to fold with traditional square origami paper, coloured on one side and white on the other, but the colours can be too harsh for some designs and the paper is not easy to find. Instead, for practice, use writing paper, photocopy paper, typing or computer print-out paper. For two-tone effect, use giftwrap paper. For display work, experiment with as wide a range of papers as you can find, or make your own surface with pastels, inks, or the like. All too often in origami, paper is seen merely as stuff to fold, not as a material in its own right that can enhance a design. So choose your papers with care.

The equipment needed for most constructions is shown in the box, right.

Equipment checklist
1 papers
2 rule
3 glue stick
4 craft knife
5 pencil

Symbols are the core of any description of origami. In recent decades the system of diagrammatic notation has become virtually standardized throughout the world, so that diagrams can be understood whatever the language of the book. Some of the symbols are obvious and others will be easily remembered with practice. Fold the technical examples and designs that follow, consulting this table when you see an unfamiliar symbol.

How to fold
Work on a clean, hard, level surface. Fold with meticulous care, particularly in the early creases – if they are incorrectly placed, every crease that follows will be out of alignment. Crease firmly. Look at one diagram and its symbols, then look ahead to the next diagram to see what the next shape will be. Never refer to one diagram in isolation.

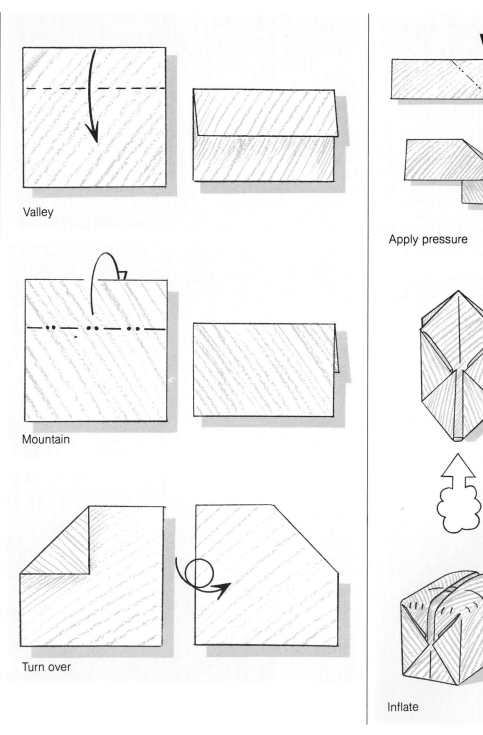

Valley

Mountain

Turn over

Apply pressure

Inflate

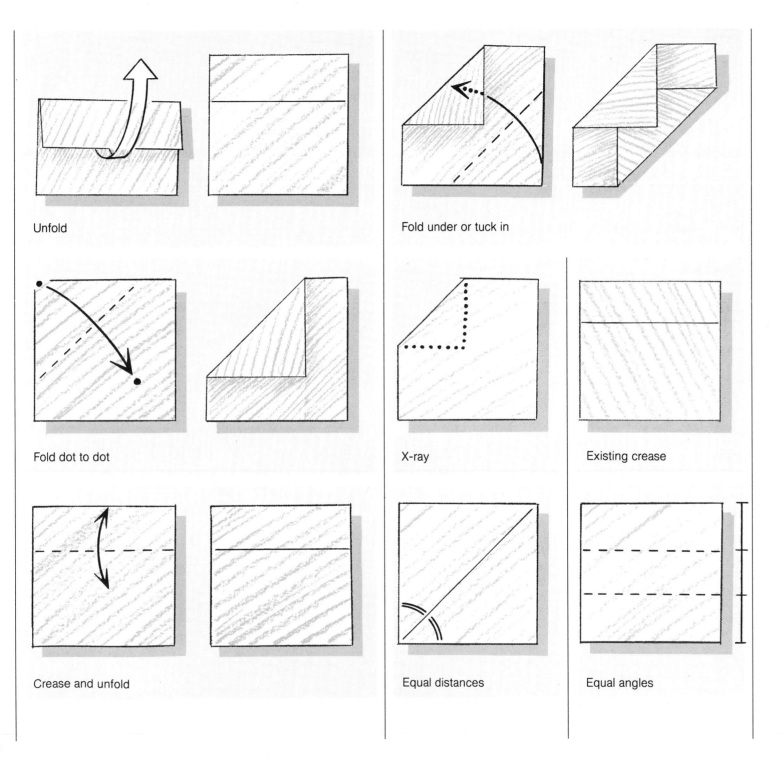

Unfold

Fold under or tuck in

Fold dot to dot

X-ray

Existing crease

Crease and unfold

Equal distances

Equal angles

The techniques that follow form the basis of origami design. However, they are all subject to an almost infinite range of subtle interpretations, so it is important to concentrate on the general principles of each technique and not to feel bound by the specific formations shown. Indeed, the more skilled the origami artist becomes, the more the distinctions between techniques begin to blur.

No list of techniques can be definitive – and that is part of origami's appeal. Virtually every new design can claim to introduce a fresh method, or invent a variant, sub-variant, reversal or inversion of an existing one, much as each game of chess can be said to have at least one new point of technical interest.

The best way to start is to practise the techniques and become familiar with the condensed diagrammatic notations. Then as you perfect your manipulative skill you will also come to recognize the different techniques shown in the diagrams.

Valley/mountain

Valley and mountain folds are the two elementary origami creases and are the counterpart of each other: a valley is a mountain seen from the reverse side of the paper. Valley folds are much easier for the hands to form than mountain folds, so when a diagram indicates a mountain, it is often easier to turn the paper over and form it as a valley, then turn back to the front again.

It is a good idea to memorize the difference between the symbols for the two folds early on, so as not to confuse them.

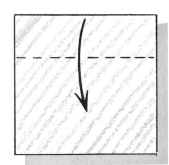

Valley

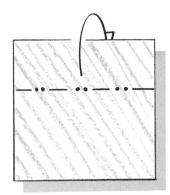

Mountain

Squash

Whereas valley/mountain folds involve the formation of just one crease at a time, squash folding and other techniques involve the simultaneous formation of several creases. Here is the basic squash fold technique:

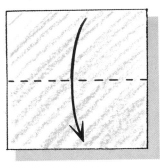

1 fold in half . . .

2 . . . and again.

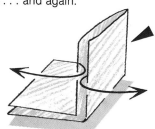

3 Apply pressure.

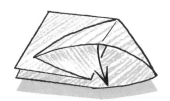

4 Squash flat.

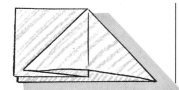

5 The squash fold complete.

Diagrammatic notation for squash fold

The above squash fold would be condensed to this:

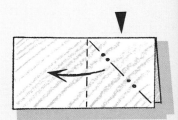

1 Squash.

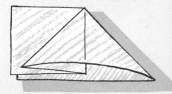

2 Complete.

Reverse fold: inside reverse

This is the most useful of all advanced origami techniques, and takes as many forms as there are designs that use it. Note that the difference between the inside reverse fold shown here and the outside reverse fold that follows it is that, in the former, the part of the paper that moves is reversed *inside* the paper, and the latter is reversed *outside*.

1 Fold in half.

Diagrammatic notation for reverse fold: inside reverse

The above manoeuvre would be condensed to this:

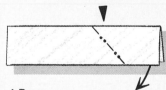

1 Reverse.

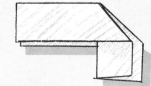

2 Complete.

2 Fold down.

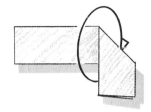

3 Swivel behind along same crease.

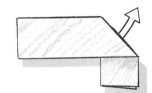

4 Unfold.

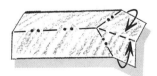

5 Form valley/mountain creases where shown and collapse flat.

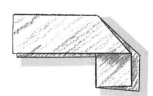

6 The inside reverse fold complete.

Squash
▲ ▲ The squash fold technique is here seen complete. The procedure may be repeated at the back of the shape.

Reverse fold: inside reverse
▲ Note the way in which the part of the paper strip which has been "reversed" has moved down *between* the layers and has turned inside out.

Reverse fold: outside reverse

Used less frequently than the inside reverse (see previous page) this is nevertheless an important technique.

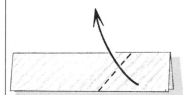

1 Fold up.

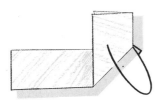

2 Swivel behind along same crease.

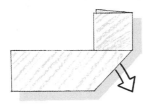

3 Unfold.

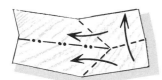

4 Form valley/mountain creases where shown and collapse flat.

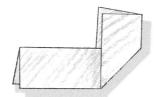

5 The outside reverse fold complete.

6 Compare this shape with the inside reverse on the previous page. They are complementary.

Diagrammatic notation for reverse fold: outside reverse

The above manoeuvre would be condensed to this:

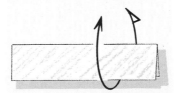

1 Outside reverse.

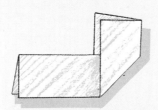

2 Complete.

Rabbit ear

The technique is so-called because the free point resembles a rabbit's ear. In a subsequent manoeuvre, that point is frequently stood upright and squashed.

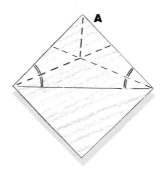

1 Crease and unfold three creases as shown.

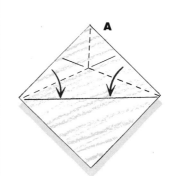

2 Fold in, lifting A.

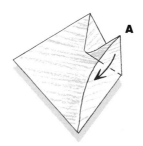

3 Flatten ear to one side.

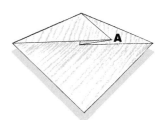

4 The rabbit ear complete.

Diagrammatic notation for rabbit ear

The above manoeuvre would be condensed to this:

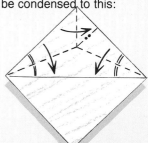

1 Rabbit ear.

2 Complete.

Sink

This is perhaps the single most complex origami technique, primarily because of the large number of creases that have to be simultaneously manipulated.

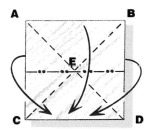

1 Collapse along marked creases.

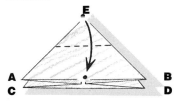

2 Fold dot to dot. Unfold.

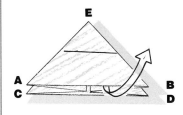

3 Open the paper.

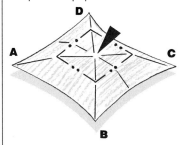

4 Crease mountains around the central square, pushing the centre down into the paper.

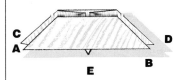

5 Collapse flat.

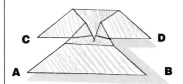

6 The sink complete.

Diagrammatic notation for sink

The above manoeuvre would be condensed to this:

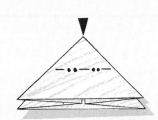

1 Sink.

2 Complete.

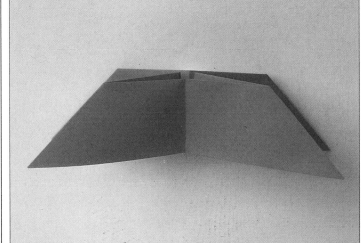

Rabbit ear

▲ ▲ The spike is here seen flattened to the right, but may also be flattened to the left. The technique may be repeated on the lower half of the sheet.

Sink

▲ In origami, any "closed" point may be inverted and sunk (or multi-sunk in a series of concentric sinks). The technique is a useful way to create long, free points.

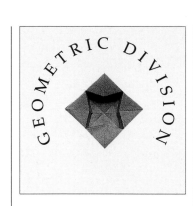

Hidden within all origami designs is a pattern of geometric creases. Most crease patterns follow simple systems, such as dividing an edge or angle into halves or quarters, but there are other systems that are more sophisticated. They separate into two categories: edge or angle division, and the folding of polygons (regular-sided shapes, such as a hexagon or octagon). No division relies on guesswork or trial and error: each is made by folding *one specific point to another* and each can be proved accurate using geometric or trigonometric theorems. They are all quick and reliable, and do not require the use of a protractor, compass, rule or pencil. More importantly, they are all supremely elegant.

Surprisingly, there is not just one way to divide an edge or fold a polygon, but many. Some methods are direct, while others are more complex, revealing unexpected and satisfying edge or crease alignments during the construction.

Edge division

To create thirds along an edge, follow this simple method.

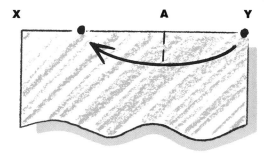

1 Fold Y towards X, estimating one-third. Pinch at A.

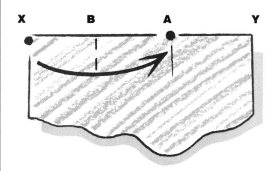

2 Fold X to pinch A, pinching at B.

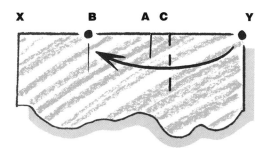

3 Fold Y to B, pinching at C (near A).

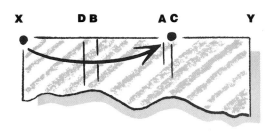

4 Fold X to C, pinching at D (near B). Repeat, folding Y, then X, then Y, then X etc across to the last pinch made, *until a pinch is made on top of an existing pinch*. That is a perfect third of edge XY.

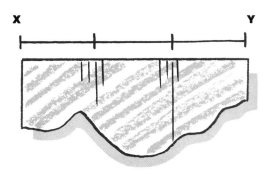

5 Similar systems, but with different XY folding patterns can be devised to fold *any* division.

Angle division

This method to divide *any* angle into thirds is closely related to the edge division technique opposite.

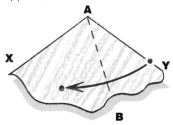

1 Angle XAY is arbitrary. Fold AY towards AX, estimating one-third. Crease AB.

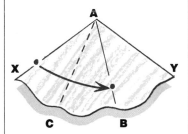

2 Fold AX to AB, creasing AC.

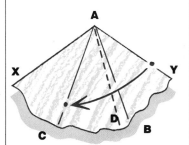

3 Fold AY to AC, creasing AD (near AB).

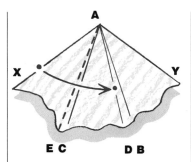

4 Fold AX to AD, creasing AE (near AC). Repeat, folding AY to AE, then folding AX to that crease, then AY to this new crease, and so on, *until a crease is made on top of an existing crease.* That is a perfect third of angle XAY.

5 Similar systems, but with different AX, AY folding patterns can be devised to fold any angle into any number of equal angles.

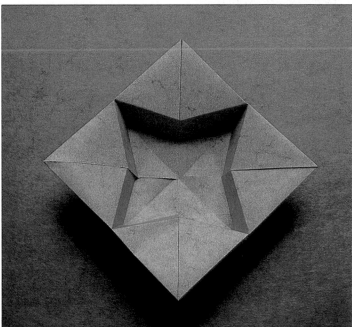

TRADITIONAL
Beak
▲ ▲ This humorous design in which the mouth opens and closes is made by the edge division method, dividing the edge into thirds. Origami purists would regard the drawn eyes as a cheat, arguing that eyes could be achieved by folding. They are correct!

PHILIP SHEN
Dish
▲ The form of this shallow dish is achieved by angle division, dividing the corners of a square into equal thirds. A further set of creases is then added and the form collapsed into shape.

Polygons: equilateral triangle

Use a rectangle of paper, creased and unfolded along the middle.

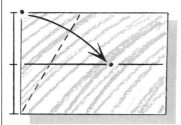

1 Pre-crease the mid-point horizontal, then fold dot to dot.

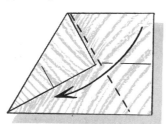

2 Fold across.

3 Unfold.

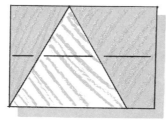

4 Cut off the excess paper. The unshaded part is the equilateral triangle.

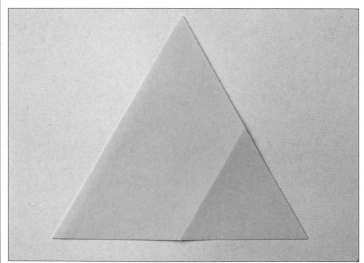

5 If the crease is considered to scar the design, it may be largely eliminated by creasing only at the step 1 location point, not along the whole length of the paper.

Polygons: hexagon

Use a square of paper, already creased and unfolded down the middle.

1 Pre-crease a horizontal mid-point, then fold the bottom edge to the top.

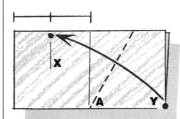

2 Pinch the three-quarter crease X. Fold corner Y to touch crease X, so that this new crease starts exactly at A.

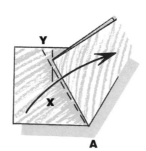

3 Fold across.

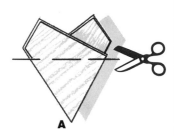

4 Cut off the excess paper and open the triangle.

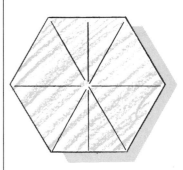

5 The complete hexagon.

6 The hexagon will be misproportioned if the cut at step 4 is incorrectly made, so make it with care. The creases are usefully placed and should not spoil a design.

Polygons: octagon

Begin with a square of paper, preferably uncreased or creased with just one of the two folds seen in step 1.

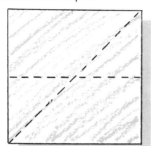

1 Pre-crease one diagonal and the horizontal.

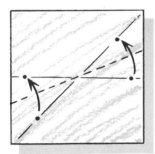

2 Align these two creases.

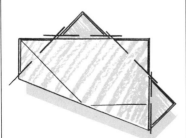

3 Cut off the triangles.

4 Open the paper.

5 The complete octagon.

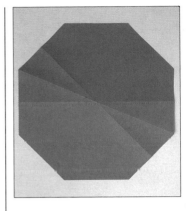

6 This is a very elegant and accurate way to fold an octagon, because the paper never becomes bulky and the triangles are easy to cut off.

TRADITIONAL
Irises

These designs have been folded from an equilateral triangle, hexagon and octagon, to make blooms with three, six or eight petals. They are all made in exactly the same way as the traditional four-petal iris folded from a square, which can be found in many origami books. It is clear that the greater the number of edges that a polygon has, the shorter the petals become. This interesting exercise can be performed on most geometric designs, such as the Pinwheel shown later in this section.

DESIGN STYLIZATION

It is one thing to understand the techniques of origami, but techniques by themselves mean little. In origami more than in any other papercraft it is important to see how the techniques relate to specific designs. That is why the remainder of this section is devoted to providing instructions for designs. These not only present the techniques described earlier but also relate the designs to major origami styles and themes.

In drawing, the likeness of a subject may be rendered with just a few skilled strokes of a pen. So it is with origami, but using folds. It is a demanding creative challenge to reduce a complex shape to its essential form, then to fold that form in a simple and elegant manner. Beginners frequently suppose that such "simple" origami is too elementary to be worth considering, but they often return to it after learning advanced techniques.

Not all simple or stylized origami is good. Much of it strains to be recognizable, or is mis-proportioned, or just mundane. When successful, though, it has the quality of looking "discovered", not created, of appearing obvious yet sophisticated.

PAUL JACKSON
Stylized building
Begin with a 2×1 rectangle of medium-weight paper, the same colour on both sides.

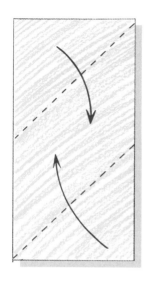

1 Fold in the top left and bottom right corners.

2 Fold the bottom triangle behind.

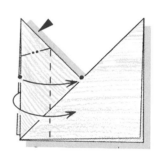

3 Pull the top layer across, squashing the top corner flat.

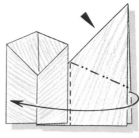

4 Similarly, but at a larger scale, pull the top layer at the right across to the left, squashing the corner.

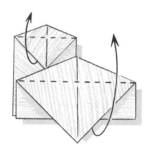

5 Fold up the loose corners.

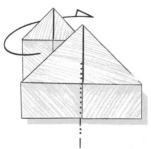

6 Along a hidden crease, fold the smaller triangle behind to stand perpendicular to the main face.

7 The building complete. Though simple, the design is very three-dimensional.

SEIRYO TAKEKAWA
Mount Fuji and the sea
Begin with a square of two-tone paper, coloured on one side and white on the reverse.

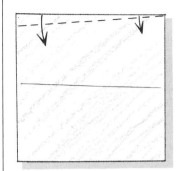

1 Fold down the top edge, a little more at the left than at the right.

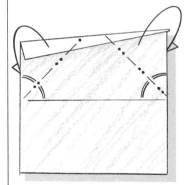

2 Fold the sides behind to lie level with the centre crease.

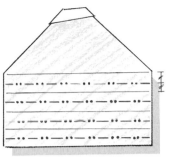

3 Divide the lower half into quarters, all with valley folds.

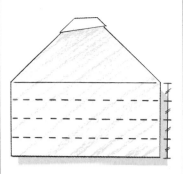

4 Place mountain folds between the valleys to create a zigzag pleat.

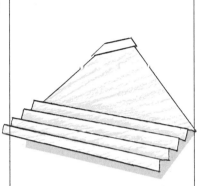

5 *Mount Fuji and the sea* complete.

The aim of technology folding is to design folded representations of subjects that might at first seem impossibly complex by the "rules" of the art, or to fold traditional subjects in greater detail. It is a puzzle-solver's approach to origami, more akin to engineering than craft, and has been the predominant style in the West since the 1960s. Recently it has also become popular in Japan.

Some of its achievements are extraordinary, such as Max Hulme's one-piece chessboard from a paper square white on one side and coloured on the reverse, or Robert Lang's one-piece, three-dimensional cuckoo clock, complete with all the traditional Swiss trimmings, including a cuckooing bird. Both – of course – are uncut.

Such remarkable detail is achieved in one of two ways. Firstly, by developing techniques to liberate as many free points from the paper as are required for a particular subject (say for tusks, fingers, or a full set of insect's legs), then to manoeuvre them to the correct position. Secondly, by covering a sheet with a grid of squares, then using those creases and carefully placed

diagonals to collapse the sheet into a series of box shapes. This technique is particularly appropriate for the representation of man-made objects, such as vehicles and household items, though it is also used to represent animals. The design here uses the second technique.

Stephenson's rocket (engine)
MAX HULME
Begin with a large square of paper. Two-tone paper will create wheels of a different colour. Paper-backed metallic foil will hold a better shape than paper, but can look garish.

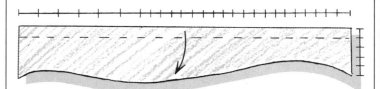

1 Divide the square into a 32 × 32 grid of accurate squares. This is best done by folding in half, unfolding, finding quarters by folding the edges to the centre crease, unfolding, finding eighths by folding the edges to each quarter crease, then finding sixteenths and subsequently thirty-seconds in a similar way, unfolding each new crease. This takes quite a while, even for an expert, but be precise. Then fold in an edge along the first crease. Repeat at the opposite edge.

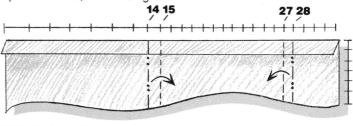

2 Pleat where shown.

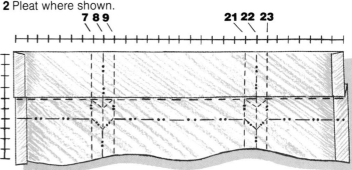

3 Make the paper three-dimensional (look at step 4 for help) by collapsing where shown. Note the short diagonals.

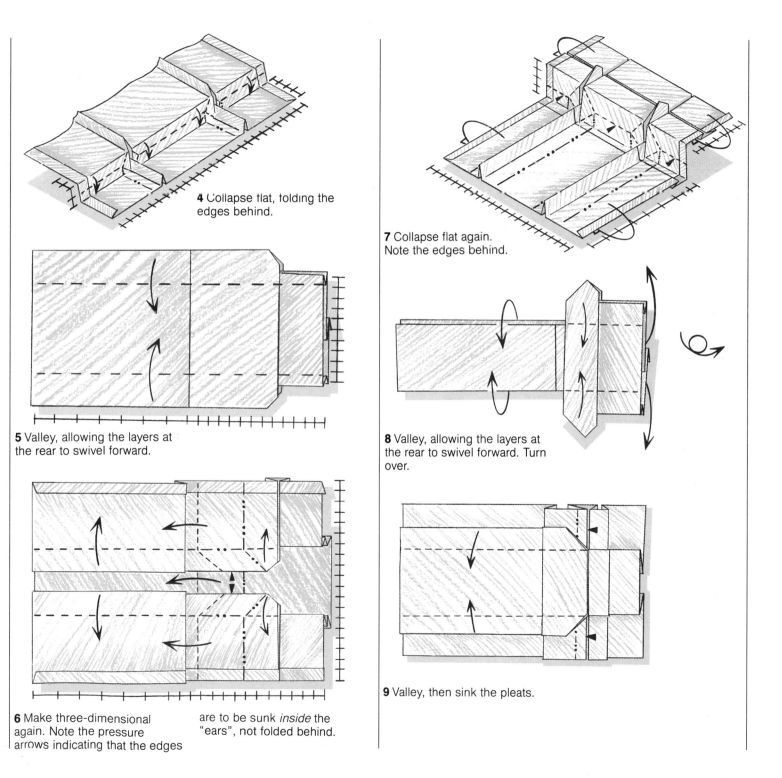

4 Collapse flat, folding the edges behind.

5 Valley, allowing the layers at the rear to swivel forward.

6 Make three-dimensional again. Note the pressure arrows indicating that the edges are to be sunk *inside* the "ears", not folded behind.

7 Collapse flat again. Note the edges behind.

8 Valley, allowing the layers at the rear to swivel forward. Turn over.

9 Valley, then sink the pleats.

10 To prepare the front wheels, open the two pleats to a box shape, then . . .

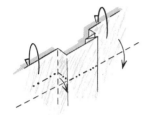

11 . . . collapse as shown, forming a horizontal lip.

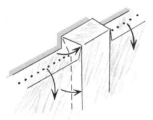

12 Swivel the sides around to the right.

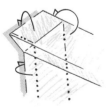

13 Squash the box flat. Note the shape of step 14. Repeat steps 10-13 with the other front wheel. Repeat steps 10-13 with the smaller rear wheels, but forming smaller boxes.

14 Form valley folds top and bottom, swivelling the edges. Fold in half.

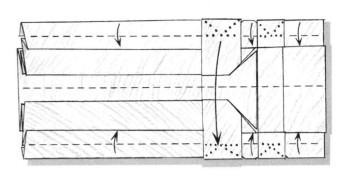

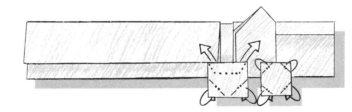

15 Lift out the tops of the front wheels. Round off all the wheels.

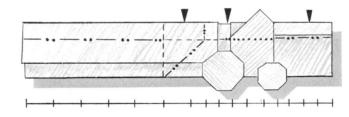

16 Make three-dimensional. Begin the chimney.

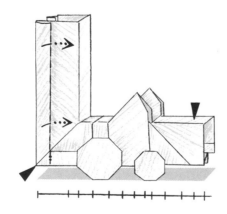

17 Tuck in the front edges of the chimney. Collapse the footplate.

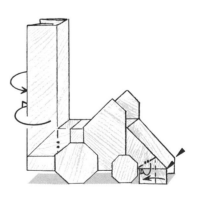

18 Interlock the front edges of the chimney. Narrow the back of the footplate.

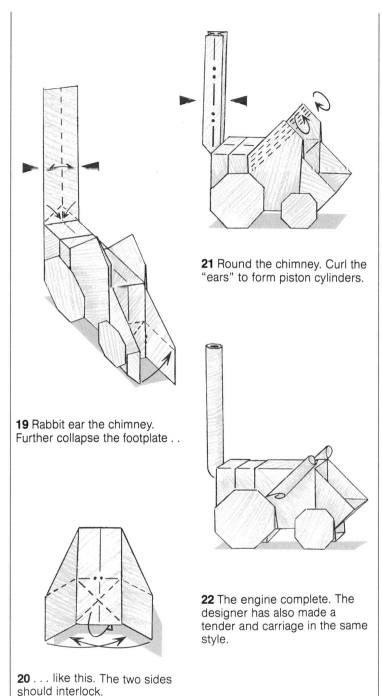

19 Rabbit ear the chimney. Further collapse the footplate . .

20 . . . like this. The two sides should interlock.

21 Round the chimney. Curl the "ears" to form piston cylinders.

22 The engine complete. The designer has also made a tender and carriage in the same style.

The engine complete.

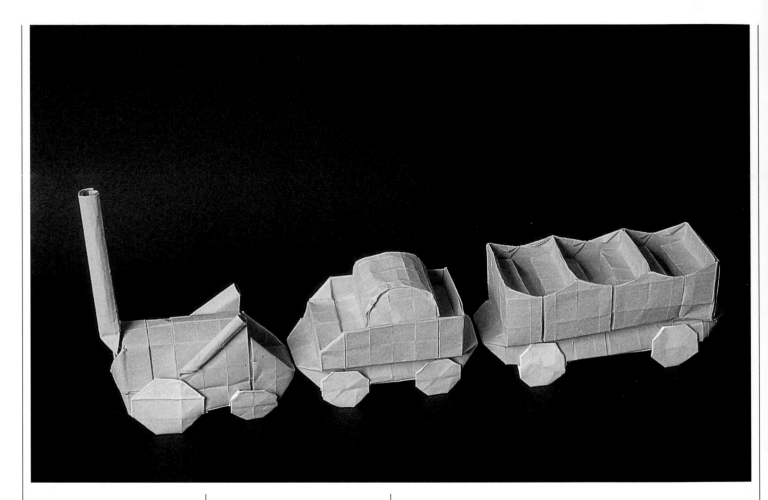

Here is the engine again, complete with its tender and carriage. Similar techniques to free the wheels are used in all three pieces and all three are folded from a grid of squares which are ingeniously collapsed into box shapes with additional diagonals. The curvature of the water tank is achieved by carefully pushing in the corners of an upturned box.
Engine length: 20cm (8in).

DESIGN : MODULES

Modular folding is a particular genre of origami in which identically folded units lock together without glue to create larger shapes. Some modular systems are two-dimensional, but most of them are three-dimensional, locking to form Platonic or Archimedean solids and their stellated or truncated variants. Only a few systems offer brick-like, open-ended creativity for the folder: the majority of modules are designed to make specific solids.

What may seem to be an austere backwater of origami has yielded an immense number of elegant designs. The appeal is a satisfying mix of geometry, colour patterns and simple folding. There is also a strong sense of the whole being more than the parts, of a spectacular structure made with little effort.

Cubeoctahedron
TOMOKO FUSE
Begin with six 2 × 1 rectangles of thin or medium-weight paper, divided into three colour pairs. All the modules are folded identically.

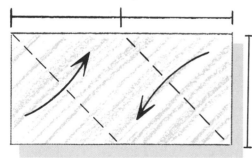

1 Fold up the bottom left-hand corner, and fold down the top right-hand corner. When folding the other modules, always fold these two corners.

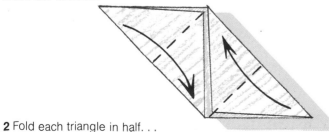

2 Fold each triangle in half. . .

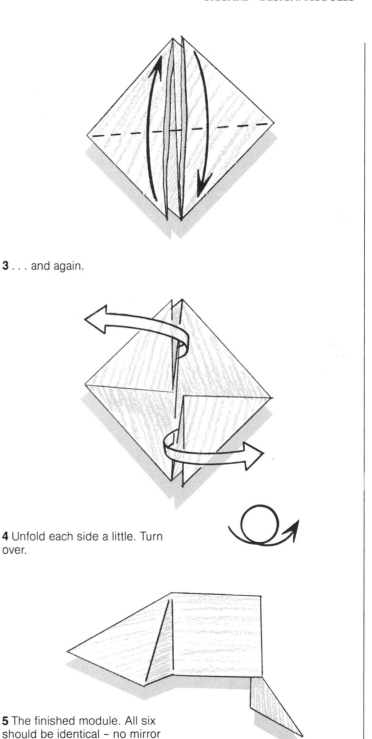

3 . . . and again.

4 Unfold each side a little. Turn over.

5 The finished module. All six should be identical – no mirror images.

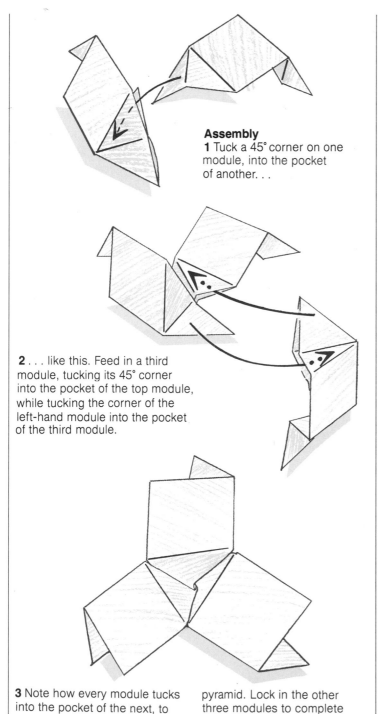

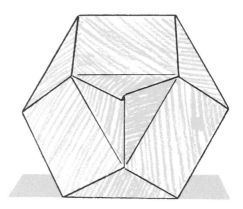

Assembly
1 Tuck a 45° corner on one module, into the pocket of another. . .

2 . . . like this. Feed in a third module, tucking its 45° corner into the pocket of the top module, while tucking the corner of the left-hand module into the pocket of the third module.

3 Note how every module tucks into the pocket of the next, to form a well-locked inverted pyramid. Lock in the other three modules to complete the design.

4 The cubeoctahedron complete. Note that it has six square faces and eight triangular faces, four of which are triangular spaces, four of which are inverted pyramids.

5 The artist has designed many ingenious modular structures. This is one of her simplest.

DAVID MITCHELL
Proteus module
This elegant example of
modular ORIGAMI is folded from
30 identical units, three of
which interlock without glue at
each small triangular face. Each
module forms part of two such
faces.
Diameter: 18cm (7in)

Most origami is non-functional, but there are a surprising number of functional designs too. Boxes are the most popular subject, some simple, others very elaborate. Turned upside-down, many boxes make excellent hats. Other origami items to wear include warm newspaper slippers, modular belts, finger rings, bracelets, floral buttonholes, necklaces and earrings. A few people make and sell origami jewellery, stiffening and waterproofing the paper with PVA and/or clear polyurethane varnish.

In the kitchen, simple leakproof cups, saucers or boxes can be folded from aluminium foil or greaseproof paper. On the dining table, decoratively folded paper or linen napkins are often seen, and origami can be used to make place-name cards, napkin rings and take-away bags.

For Christmas, many modular designs make stunning tree decorations. Mundane gifts can be presented inside decorative origami boxes.

Strong twist-flat purses can be made from cut-down milk cartons and sturdy wallets from stiff paper coated with PVA. There are many origami

envelopes, some decorative for the presentation of letters by hand, others for practical use in the mail. So, while paper-folded objects may not have a major everyday role, they can be useful as well as attractive.

Photo frame
JOHN S SMITH
Begin with a sheet a little wider than the photo and about two-and-a-half times as high.

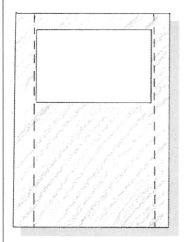

1 Place the photo centrally on the paper and fold in the long edges over the photo.

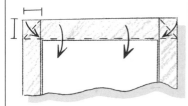

2 At the top edge, fold in the corners, then fold down the top edge.

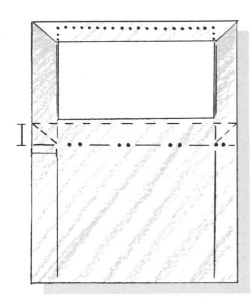

3 Pleat, as shown, at the bottom edge of the photo. Measure it carefully.

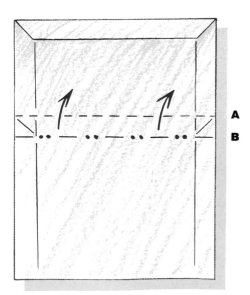

4 Form the pleat. Note A and B.

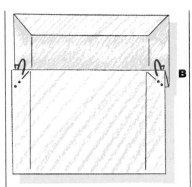

5 Fold in corner B. Pleat at the other side.

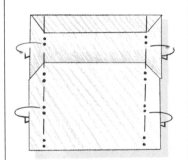

6 Fold behind, along step 1 creases.

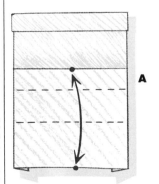

7 Crease across at A. Unfold. Fold dot to dot. Unfold.

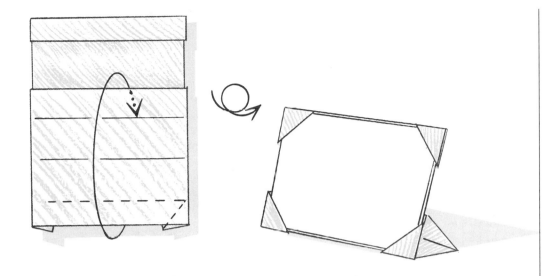

8 Crease across near the bottom edge, in such a position that when the bottom edge tucks into the pocket, the frame leans slightly backwards. Bend in the bottom corners to aid the tuck. Turn over.

9 The photo frame complete. Tuck the photo behind the corner triangles. Note that this design is made using only valley/mountain folds.

Action models are designs to play with. Many children know a few such designs, such as the paper dart or fortune teller (operated by inserting the thumb and forefinger of both hands into its four pockets and moving them together and apart to reveal two different sets of faces upon which numerals and fortunes have been written). Other designs such as the noisy Banger! and anarchic waterbomb are less well-known today than in earlier times.

This genre of origami, though, is not confined to the classroom. The traditional Japanese flapping bird (whose wings flap when its tail is pulled) has been known to the West since the 1860s and is widely regarded by experts as being perhaps the finest of all origami designs, Indeed, quality action designs are widely collected, perhaps because more than any other genre of origami they are the embodiment of "a good idea". A design which jumps, spins, flaps, winks, tumbles, talks, balances, makes a noise or flies is easy to admire and enjoy.

There are a surprising number of action designs; indeed, some creators specialise in them. The most popular subject is undoubtedly paper aircraft, to which an entire bookshelf may be devoted. The traditional paper dart is the best known, but there is an astonishing variety of flying craft, some very complex or abstract. Joint second in popularity are flapping birds and jumping frogs – many contemporary designers have created their own examples, though some are wagglers and shufflers rather than flappers and jumpers.

At their best, action models are the most easily appreciated, most original, most ingeniously designed and most entertaining of all origami designs. They are neither childish nor banal.

PHILIP SHEN
Pinwheel

Begin with a 15–20cm (6–8in) equilateral triangle of thin paper .

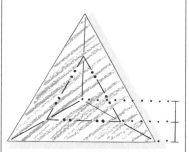

1 Crease from the corners *only as far as the centre point.*

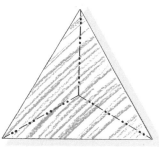

2 Make mountain creases parallel to the edges, midway between the edges and the centre point. Do not crease beyond the existing creases.

3 Fold dot to dot, but make a valley crease *only* where shown. Do not make it longer.

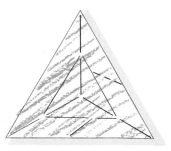

4 Repeat with the other two corners to create a symmetrical crease pattern.

5 The creasing is now complete. Strengthen all the creases, twisting the edges behind where shown. Push in the junctions of the valley and mountain creases at three points around the triangle. Do all three at the same time. Note that parts of the step 2 creases *do not form*. Persevere!

6 This is the basic pinwheel form. Turn over.

7 The centre point, about which three edges rotate, stands up. Push the centre point *down into the body of the design* to create. . .

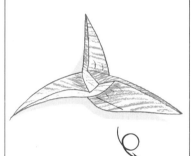

8 . . . a concave centre, locked into shape. Turn over.

9 The pinwheel complete – a beautiful shape from only nine creases. To make it spin, straighten a paper clip and insert one end through the back. Push it forward to touch the nose. Hold the protruding end of wire and push the pinwheel through the air. Alternatively, if the paper is very thin, spin the pinwheel by dropping it from a height.

POP-UPS

INCISED POP-UPS

MULTI-PIECE POP-UPS

Pop-ups were first used in children's books during the latter half of the nineteenth century, though books with parts such as lift-up window flaps were used as far back as the thirteenth century. The high cost of production and an uncertain world economy saw the decline of this expensive book form during the first half of the twentieth century. In the late 1950s and 1960s, innovative pop-up books from Czechoslovakia were translated into English, which inspired American designers and publishers to create their own. In turn, their work influenced British designers, and both countries have since produced many remarkable pop-up books and greetings cards.

It is easy to see why pop-ups have such an enduring fascination: they are often extraordinarily ingenious, combining the rigours of geometry with the appeal of magic. At a deeper level, the transformation from two dimensions to three and back defies our everyday experience and seems barely possible.

The basic techniques for incised pop-ups and MULTI-PIECE POP-UPS, described here, are not complex, but when put together in combination they can create designs of remarkable intricacy. As with ORIGAMI, every new design introduces a technical nuance and therefore the variations of technique are endless.

Materials

Roughs can be made using medium-weight paper. Finished examples, though, should be made with thin, springy card. Use a strong paper glue or general-purpose adhesive, such as PVA. Stick glues are fine for roughs but are not strong enough for finished work.

Construction

All pop-ups must be made very carefully, or they will not collapse flat. Roughs can be made as quickly as necessary but finished examples need to be made slowly, using a rule, protractor, and occasionally a template. Several roughs may be needed before a finished design can be attempted.

Explore the techniques that follow by copying examples from the book and by inventing your own variations. If you have any pop-up books to hand, look through them and try to identify the mechanisms that make them work, many of which are explained here.

Symbols

///// = glue strip.

For an explanation of the other symbols used in this section, see page 20-21.

Equipment checklist
1 card
2 protractor
3 rule
4 craft knife
5 pencil
6 glue
7 cutting mat
8 scissors

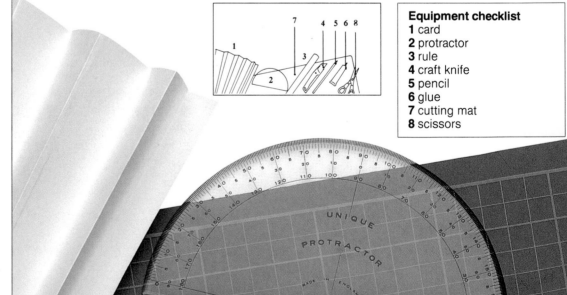

INCISED POP-UPS

Incised pop-ups are pop-ups constructed from one sheet of card that has been slit and creased. The card opens to 90° to reveal the pop-ups; as it is opened further, the pop-ups flatten back into the card. Adhesive is seldom used, except perhaps to glue a completed design to a backing sheet for strength.

A well thought-out, well-made incised pop-up – even a simple one – can be of an elegance unsurpassed by any other papercraft technique, and its secret lies in care over basic principles.

There is one tip that will save you a lot of time: if you make a slit in the wrong place, do not discard the sheet to start afresh. Instead, seal the slit by placing sticky tape over it at the back of the sheet, then slit again in the correct position. That way, a slit may be made, taped up and re-made many times.

2 The single slit pop-up complete. Note the arrangement of the valley/mountain creases.

Single slit: basic example
1 Cut in from the crease, then fold the triangles backwards and forwards along the two creases. Open the card and pull the triangles upwards, re-creasing the central fold as a mountain. Fold the card in half and press flat, to reinforce the creases.

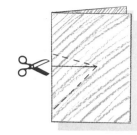

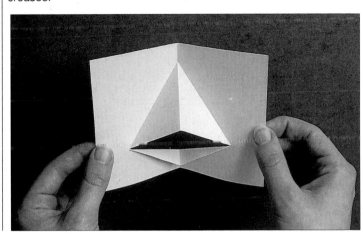

Single slit: variations

The slit can start anywhere along the length of the central crease and can take any shape. The secondary creases can come away from the end of the slit at any angle.

Note the shallow angle of the crease. The finished piece is shown below.

Here, the pop-up will pierce the plane of the card. The finished piece is shown below.

The crease may, as here, run off the bottom edge. The finished piece is shown below.

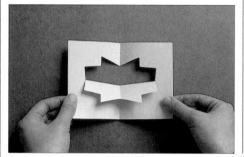

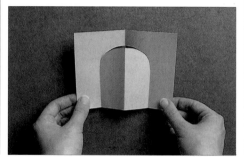

Double slit: basic example

The technique is very similar to the single slit left, but offers greater creative possibilities.

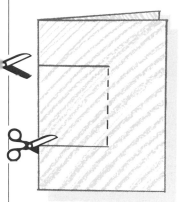

1 Cut in twice from the central crease, then fold the loose section that lies between the slits backwards and forwards. Open the card and pull that loose section towards you, re-creasing the central fold on the "belt" as a mountain. Fold the card in half and press flat to reinforce the creases.

2 The pop-up is complete. Note the single mountain crease among four valleys.

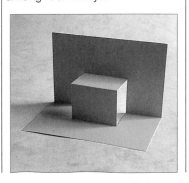

Double slit: variations

As with the single slit technique, the slits can be any shape, though the secondary crease must always connect the ends.

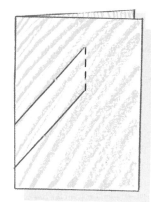

A V-shaped double slit. The slits need not be parallel.

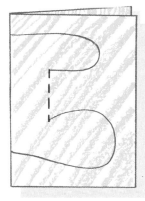

This complex variation pierces the plane of the card to create a "front and back" effect.

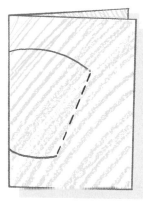

Note that the crease between the ends of the slits is not parallel to the centre crease.

Asymmetric: basic example

The previous single and double slit examples and variations will all produce symmetrical pop-ups. This is because the card is first folded in half to form a double layer, then cut through both layers to create a slit that is the same shape on both sides of the crease. With careful measurement, however, the symmetry can be broken to make possible a much wider vocabulary of form.

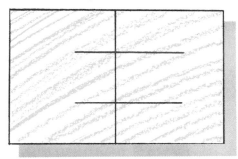

1 Form *no creases,* but make a measured drawing. Draw the central crease, then draw the two slits.

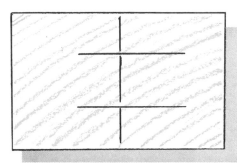

2 Draw two valley creases, parallel to the central crease.

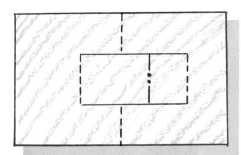

3 Measure the distance from the central crease to the *nearer* valley crease line. Reproduce that distance to the inside of the other valley crease. This will be the position of the mountain crease.

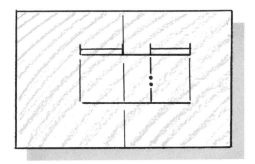

4 Erase that part of the central crease that runs across the pop-up "belt." Cut the slits, make the creases (either by hand or by scoring, depending on the weight of the paper or card) and fold to shape.

5 This is the result, if all the creases are correctly placed. It is critical to understand which distances are equal – and why – if this useful technique is to be mastered. If you are still unsure of the principles, have a go at remaking this example.

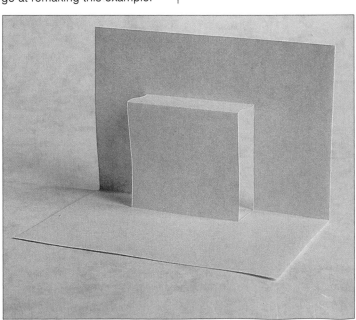

Asymmetric: variations

The only rule here is that the two valleys and one mountain that make the pop-up must all be parallel to the central crease. Before making any creases, draw everything as described below, measuring carefully.

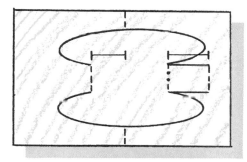

Asymmetric principles are used here to create a form which extends "behind" the plane of the card.

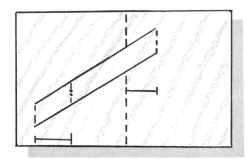

Note the equal distances here and how they are measured horizontally, not at the angle of the band.

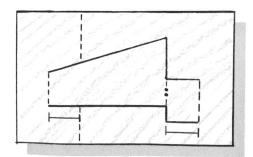

Here, the shorter plane extends below the longer one, placing the mountain crease between two distinct shapes and not in a seemingly arbitrary position.

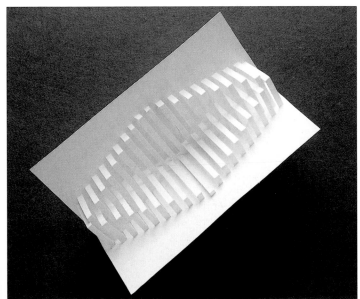

▲ ▲ The three asymmetric variations are here shown photographed. Careful measurement and a clear constructional procedure are the keys to the successful creative use of this technique.

PAUL JACKSON
Pop-up
▲ This intricate incised pop-up uses asymmetric pop-up techniques to create a negative/positive diamond form.
Length: 6in (15cm)

Non-parallel creases

Whatever shapes the techniques shown so far may form, the creases will always be parallel and somewhat box-like. Here is a way to construct creases which are not parallel but tapered, creating odd perspective effects. A protractor will be needed.

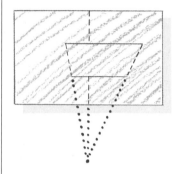

1 The slits are of unequal length, but the creases meet at an imaginary focal point below the card, on the line of the central crease. Draw everything before slitting or creasing.

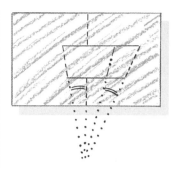

2 To locate the position of the mountain crease, measure the *smaller* angle between one valley crease and the central crease, then measure the same angle to the inside of the other valley crease. The mountain crease must also radiate from the focal point. When the construction is complete, slit, crease, and fold to shape.

3 The construction complete. With this technique, it is usually easier and more accurate to form the creases by scoring the paper or card, rather than creasing by hand.

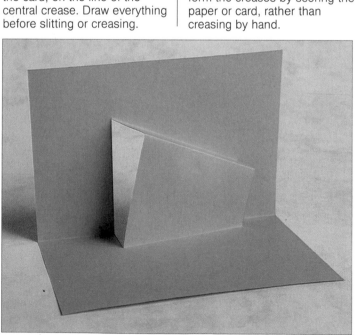

Generations: basic example

Every pop-up is built around an existing crease, and generates its own new creases. These new creases can in turn be used to create more pop-ups, which in turn generate new creases that can be used to create more pop-ups. . . and so on, down through successive generations.

The principle can be applied to any of the above techniques, or to different techniques at each generation.

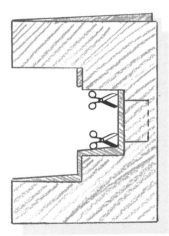

1 Begin with the basic example of the double slit pop-up, fully formed. Make two cuts into the nearside folded edge, and proceed to make a simple double slit pop-up, identical to the bigger one just made, but smaller.

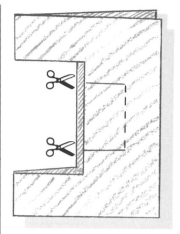

2 Similarly, now cut into the new nearside folded edge (the one just made), to make another double slit pop-up. This process can continue through the generations, until creases become too small for pop-ups to be formed. Generations can also be cut into central mountain creases to form what might be termed "pop-ins", rather than pop-ups.

3 The example diagrammed above is here shown fully formed. Practise this technique.

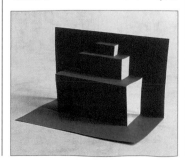

Generations: variations

This sequence of photographs (right) shows how a complex form can be built up generation by generation. The form here is symmetrical, but the principle can equally be applied to asymmetric forms that are drawn before being cut.

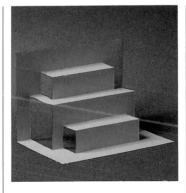

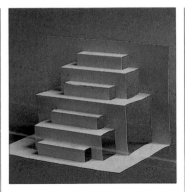

1 This shows the first generation.

2 Cutting through all the layers of the first generation pop-up, to create the top and bottom "steps".

3 The third generation is formed by cutting through all the layers of the second generation.

PAUL JACKSON
Head
This piece uses the generations technique. The hair pleats are made in three generations and the eyes built up from the second generation valleys that run down through them. The ears are snipped free, but do not pop up.
Height: 30cm (12in)

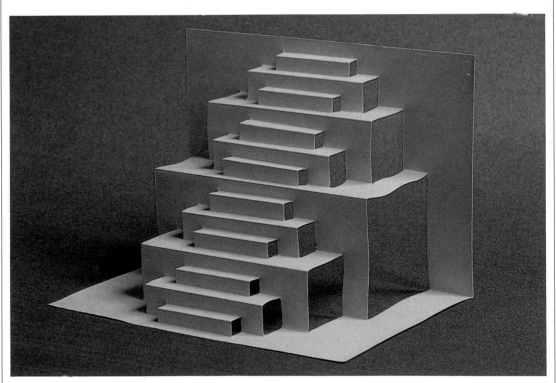

4 The pop-up is now complete – the card will not take a doubling of the "steps" with another generation. The large number of creases means that the form takes some force to pull open, but once erected will not wilt shut as pop-ups with few creases frequently do.

Cut-aways: basic example

No matter how elegant and sophisticated the pop-ups created by the techniques already shown, the straight lines of the creases will always produce block-like forms. The cut-away technique releases the paper to one side of a crease to create interesting, free-standing forms.

1 Make the double slit basic example pop-up . Open it out flat. Incise a semi-circular line that begins and ends on the left-hand valley crease and incise a rectangular line that begins and ends on the central mountain crease. Re-form the pop-up, but do not crease inside each incision, allowing the semi-circular and rectangular forms to stand proud.

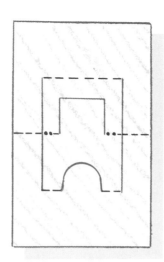

2 The basic example complete. The cut-away technique is the single most useful of all incised pop-up techniques. It transforms conventional pop-up shapes – which are frequently static and heavy-looking – into forms that are lighter and more dynamic. `

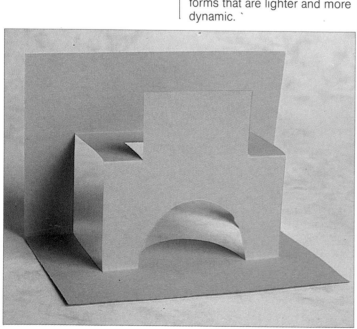

Cut-aways: variations

The application of cut-away techniques is almost infinite, because any shape can be made to project from any crease, as long as the shapes do not collide or leave so little of a crease that the structure becomes very weak. They can be used with any previously described technique or combination of techniques. For finished works, draw the slits and creases onto uncreased card, thereby avoiding creases across the base of all free-standing shapes, then slit and crease.

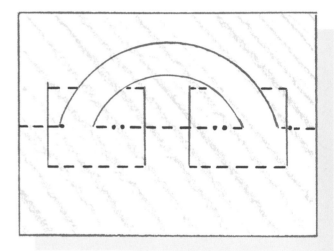

The cut-away arch bridges the gap between two conventional double slit pop-ups, leaving an interesting negative shape.

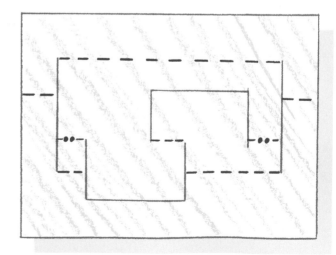

Here, two cut-aways originate from the same crease, and overlap. The result is a pleasing double cut-away form, projecting forward at each side of the mountain crease.

The completed cut-aways. Note the interior spaces created by this technique. They add a lightness to a pop-up form and make possible an infinite range of silhouettes.

KEIKO NAKAZAWA
Business card
The pop-up is a one-piece design, formed from the central arms of a sheet of paper pleated in the shape of a letter W, the outer arms being glued flat to a sheet of backing card. Though one-piece, it could also have been made from two pieces (one for the dog, one for the backing card) using the multi-piece upturned V technique.
11×9×4.5cm (4$\frac{1}{2}$×3$\frac{3}{4}$×2in)

Multi-piece pop-ups are pop-ups made from many pieces of shaped card, stuck to a backing sheet that opens and closes to reveal or enclose the pop-up. Whereas with INCISED POP-UPS the backing sheet opens to 90° for effect, with multi-piece designs it opens flat, to 180°.

The technique requires more construction than before but creates forms that are more sculptural. Roughs can be made from medium- or heavyweight paper, but finished works should be constructed from thin, springy card. The backing sheet may need to be a heavy card, or even board, depending on the stresses imposed by the pop-up. Remember to use a good strong adhesive for the finished construction, applying glue sparingly to the tabs.

PAUL JOHNSON
Book
This is a multi-piece pop-up, using techniques derived from incised generations techniques. 40×30×30cm (16×12×12in)

Horizontal V: basic example
This is the simplest 180° pop-up technique.

1 Cut out a rectangle of medium- or heavyweight paper. Crease it down the centre, then crease it across the bottom. Make a short slit at the bottom edge to separate two tabs.

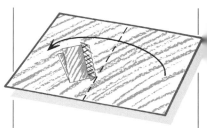

2 Fold the paper oblong in half, so that the tabs are to the outside. Apply glue to each tab. Stick one tab to the backing sheet, so that the central crease on the backing sheet *touches* the crease on the pop-up. Fold the other half of the backing sheet on top, so that it sticks to the other tab.

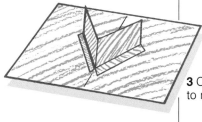

3 Open out the backing sheet to reveal the pop-up.

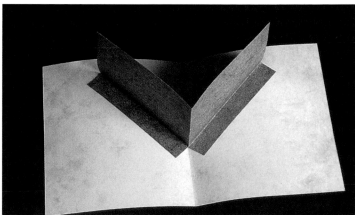

4 The basic example complete. The key here is to make the crease on the backing sheet lie exactly beneath the crease on the pop-up.

Horizontal V: variations

Almost every element here is variable, so long as the pop-up crosses the crease on the backing sheet. For example: the crease on the pop-up can move to one side of the rectangle of paper; the oblong can be any size; the V-shaped angle across the crease on the backing sheet can be anything between 1° and about 175° (but not completely straight); the crease across the bottom of the pop-up shape need not be at 90° to the vertical crease; the angles of the V either side of the crease on the backing sheet need not be the same.

The examples shown on this page will give you some ideas for variations.

The three dimensional examples are here shown photographed. Note the variety of forms made possible by changing the angle between the arms of the V.

The letter B. In this example the arms of the V are folded back against each other, so that the V is shut tight. The tabs run along the crease on the backing sheet

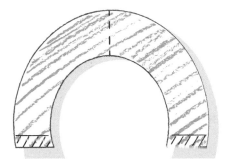

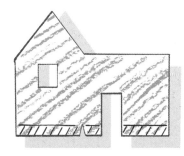

An arch. Note the angle of the crease at the base of the arch, which is almost perpendicular to the central crease on the backing sheet.

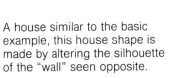

A house similar to the basic example, this house shape is made by altering the silhouette of the "wall" seen opposite.

Upturned V: basic example

This is similar to the horizontal V technique, except that now the V goes up and over the crease on the backing sheet, not flat across it.

1 Cut out an oblong of paper. Make a mountain crease across the middle and two valleys across the ends.

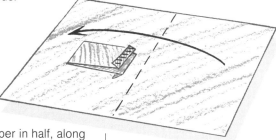

2 Fold the paper in half, along the mountain. Fold back the tabs and apply glue to each tab. Stick one tab to a backing sheet of card, parallel to, but a little way away from, the crease on the backing sheet. Fold the other half of the sheet on top, to stick to the other tab.

3 Open out the sheet to reveal the pop-up. The technique is a very effective way to achieve height in a pop-up.

Upturned V: variations

As with the horizontal V, almost every element is variable. For example: the oblong of paper can be any size; the V can become an X; the V can be placed asymmetrically on the backing sheet; the tab creases need not be parallel to the crease on the backing sheet.

Use the examples on this page as a basis for your own ideas.

Two pieces interlocked at the slits create an X-shaped pop-up, the form may – of course – be made considerably more complex than the simple example shown here.

Here, the angle of the tabs tapers. If the creases were extended, they would meet exactly at the central crease. For this reason the pop-up has to be precisely placed on the backing sheet.

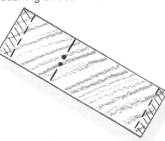

The mountain crease need not be placed in the centre of the pop-up, but can be placed to one side.

The three diagrammed examples are here shown photographed. Remember to apply adhesive sparingly to the tabs: too much will glue the pop-up flat!

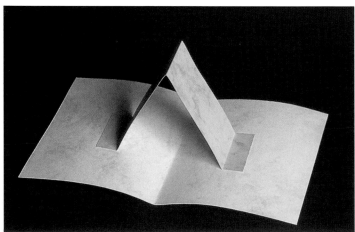

Layering: basic example

This technique provides a series of raised horizontal planes like the tiers of a wedding cake.

1 Construct three identical pillars, creased as above. Apply glue to the entire surface, then fold in half.

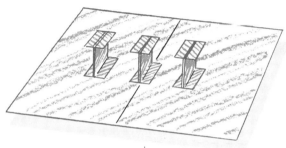

2 Glue the pillars to a backing sheet of stiff card, one along the crease on the card and one to each side, parallel to the crease. Cut out a rectangle of paper and glue it to the tops of the pillars. The paper must have a crease directly over the central pillar.

3 The basic example complete. Carefully made, the layer will be surprisingly stable and the pillars will remain pleasingly upright.

Layering: variations

The rule here is that there must be at least three supporting pillars: one along the crease on the backing sheet and one to each side, parallel to that crease. The rectangular layer can be any shape; the pillars need not be symmetrically distributed; the completed layer can be used as the base for more layers on top, or as a base for other 180° pop-up techniques.

Here are some more examples to inspire your own.

The asymmetry of the shape means that a wider pillar will need to be built under the wider side of the shape.

With complex constructions, the key is to work layer by layer, making sure that each layer can fold flat before moving upwards to the next.

Here, four pillars are used: two along the central crease and one to each side.

The three diagrammed examples are here photographed. Layering is the most sculptural of all pop-up techniques, and the most illusory (the layers appear to be unsupported).

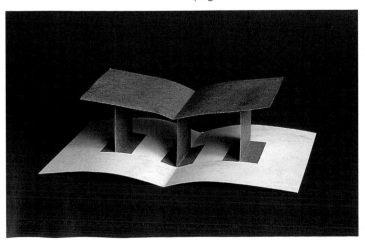

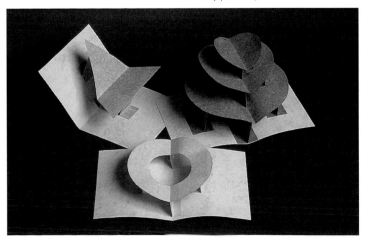

Boxes

The two basic box techniques described here show how to construct enclosed forms. They can be placed on any crease that opens 180°. The sides make a 90° angle with the backing sheet, which can be the support for any 90° or incised techniques.

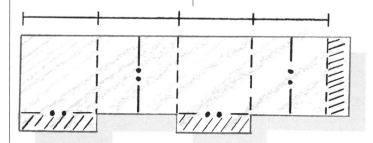

Square-on box

1 Cut out the above shape, creating tabs where shown. Glue the end tab to the opposite end of the strip to create a square tube.

2 Glue the lower tabs to a backing sheet. The two mid-face creases on the box should be directly above the crease on the backing sheet when the box is pulled open to stand square.

Square-on box: variations

1 The box may be elongated to become wider, deeper or higher. Some of the creases can be added or removed to create boxes of other shapes, such as hexagons and cylinders. A lid may be added, fastening it to the box by tabs that stick to the same faces as the lower tabs.

Below are two examples from which to adapt your own variations.

2 The boxes complete. Structures with an odd number of sides (triangles, pentagons, etc) are more complex to construct, but are a good technical exercise for the novice paper engineer.

Hexagon

Cylinder

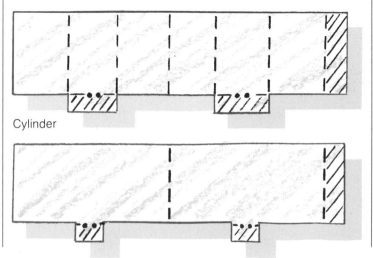

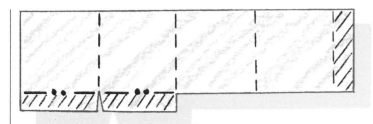

Diagonal box

1 Cut out the above shape. Glue the end tab to the opposite end of the strip to create a square tube.

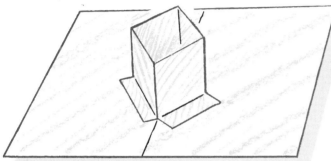

2 Glue the lower tabs to a backing sheet, one each side of the central crease, so that the crease on the backing sheet lies exactly beneath the diagonal of the box. To make a box with 90° corners, glue the tabs at 45° to the central crease. The diagonal box is perhaps a more elegant structure than previous boxes, because it holds its shape better.

Non-square boxes can be made if the tabs are not glued at 45° to the central crease.

Lid

1 To create a lid, make two identical lid sections as shown. Note the creases and tabs. Glue one to the two faces of the box already tabbed to the backing sheet, and the other to the other two faces. The two lid halves will interlock when the backing sheet is opened and the box formed.

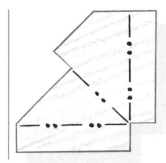

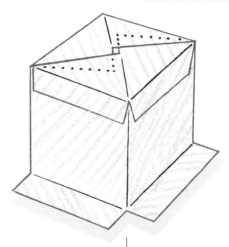

2 The diagrammed lid shown photographed.

PAPER SCULPTURE

BASIC TECHNIQUES

ARMATURES AND
ASSEMBLY

"NIGHTFLIGHT"

Throughout the centuries paper has been used in a three-dimensional form. In seventh-century China for example, paper figures were built to burn at a burial, so as to drive away evil spirits.

Sculpting in paper is just as creative as working in wood, metal or stone, and like all true art it can be practised and enjoyed at any level. Even the inexperienced can produce attractive sculptures that will give pleasure to themselves and others.

At the same time, paper sculpture has practical applications too. It is widely used in the teaching of art and design, for education generally, and in displays, exhibitions, advertising and book illustration.

Broadly speaking, paper sculptures come in two styles: the full-round sculpture, which is capable of being viewed from all sides, and the half-round, or low relief, sculpture designed to be viewed from the front only. The effect of light and shade is an important factor in the completed sculpture, and the artist will need to consider how best to exploit this when working out the original design and selecting the arrangement of the basic forms.

Equipment and materials
Paper sculpture is traditionally in white paper, and this is readily available in a range of weights (see ALL ABOUT PAPER). The best choice for the beginner is cartridge paper. Particularly large structures can be made from heavier paper but this is more difficult to work. At the other extreme, ordinary typing, computer or photocopy paper is quite suitable for small, low-relief subjects.

Coloured cartridge paper, available in a wide range of colours, makes an attractive departure from tradition. Remember, though, that coloured paper often has a sheen on one side only and you will get the best effect when light falls on the sculpture if you use the matt surface as the face side. Also, be sure to choose papers that have the colour right through; papers that are coloured on the surface only will show a white line when cut or scored.

Gold, silver and other metallic foil papers are frequently used to enhance a sculpture, but they have little or no inherent strength and need to be glued to a sheet of

cartridge paper before use. Metallic foils have no depth to their decorative surface and cannot be scored.

Gift wrapping paper also offers a host of designs for use to great effect. The paper can be backed, like foil, or designs cut out and applied to sections of a sculpture – to make a decorative cloak for an oriental figure, for example.

Mounting board, thin card (in a variety of thicknesses) and corrugated card serve as armatures and display bases. Modern foam sandwich boards (polyboards) can be especially useful, combining lightness with rigidity.

Basic equipment is inexpensive and can usually be found in the home. The only exception is the surgical scalpel with replaceable blade. The straight-edged blade is a matter of choice, but most people find a blade with a straight edge easier to use than one with a curved edge. For a specific list of tools and equipment see the checklist, right.

Optional extras

An assortment of paper clips, clothes pegs and tweezers will be invaluable for holding the work during construction. A roll of masking tape will also be useful – it can be removed easily from the work, unlike Sellotape.

Adhesives

The right glue is a must. A PVA adhesive can be used but UHU (in tubes) may be more suitable. It has the advantage of almost instantaneous adhesion and can be applied to small areas with a cocktail stick. Glue sticks, glue pens and glues marketed as suitable for children to use with paper may not be suitable for paper sculpture.

The dedicated sculptor may wish to invest in more sophisticated compasses, a set of French curves, a set square and a double-sided cutting mat. This last item will prove its worth, because its self-sealing working surface remains smooth and blades last longer.

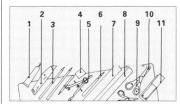

Equipment checklist
1 adhesive
2 heavy-duty trimming knife for cutting card and mounting board
3 pencils 2B and an HB for drawing and tracing
4 kneadable eraser
5 inexpensive compasses
6 scalpel
7 30cm (12in) wooden ruler This is better for applying bias to paper than a plastic rule which has too much "spring"
8 metal straight edge
9 sharp scissors (size 15cm/6in or 18cm/7in) with pointed blades
10 fine embroidery scissors for delicate work
11 small stapler – useful for hidden fastenings
12 45 × 30cm (18 × 12in) cutting board

BASIC TECHNIQUES

The essence of paper sculpture is representational shape. Beneath the shallow form of a leaf or a facial mask produced perhaps by bias, scoring and folding, it relies on the basic structural forms of cone and cylinder. Cubes and pyramids may also be used.

This section explores some of the conical and cylindrical forms and shapes which can be produced using the bending, scoring and folding techniques explained under CREASING.

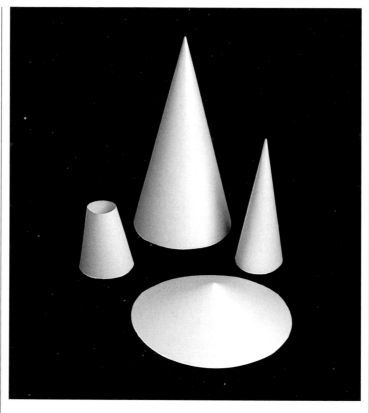

2 Cones of different diameters and heights may be produced by varying either the radius of the circle or the size of the segment which is discarded; the latter will give cones of differing diameter and height from a circle of the same size.

The cone is used in a variety of ways: it may be the body of a full-round sculpture or, in a very shallow form, for example, the eye of a low-relief figure.

Basic cones
1 Circular cones may be used to represent many things in paper sculpture and their natural rigidity makes them an ideal base on which to build. To make a cone, cut a segment from a circular piece of paper, as shown. Apply glue fully along edge A and make up the cone by overlapping edge B onto A.

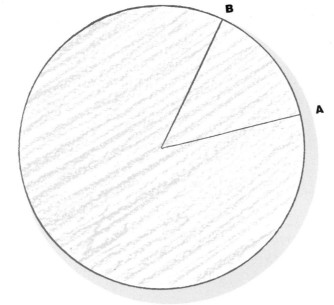

Concentric scored cones

1 All variations of this multiple scored cone are made by drawing concentric circles and scoring alternately on the face and reverse side of the paper (scores on the reverse are shown as a broken line). Each circle increases in radius by 25mm (1in) to give an overall diameter of 250mm (10in).

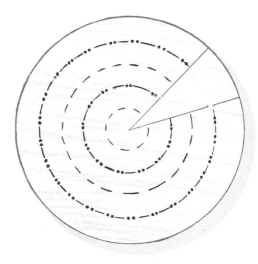

2 The largest cone was produced by removing a 30° segment, but the dimensions and the size of the segment may be varied to produce forms of different sizes.

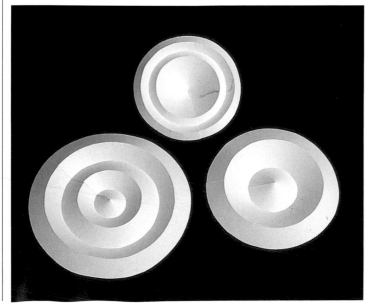

Pleated cones

1 Alternate face and reverse scores give a pleated effect with the help of accurate measurement and careful folding.

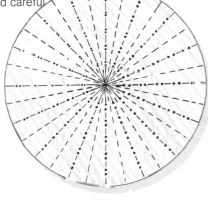

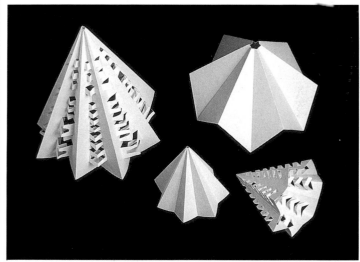

2 The larger pleated cone with decorative cut out pattern is produced from a full circle of paper 500mm (20in) in diameter. Working on the face of the paper, scores are made at 22.5° intervals. Intermediate scores are then made on the reverse side of the paper. Fourteen segments are then cut out between two reverse scores and discarded. In this particular cone the cut out surface pattern is achieved by cutting across the reverse scores only to a prepared template, but the choice of design is up to you. Gluing will be easier if a small circle is removed from the centre of the cone. The smaller pleated cone is produced from the discarded segment of the circle in a similar way, with the cut surface pattern applied to the top scores.

Scored cylinders

A rectangular biased piece of paper to the dimensions shown right, and scored, as shown, on the concave side will produce a cylinder with a recessed curved surface (see the photograph below). The paper is fastened together against the natural curve, and between the scores the curve is manipulated over a wooden dowel to achieve the fluted effect. When used in construction a scored cylinder needs to be fitted with a plain cylindrical liner for maximum strength.

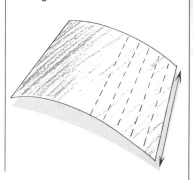

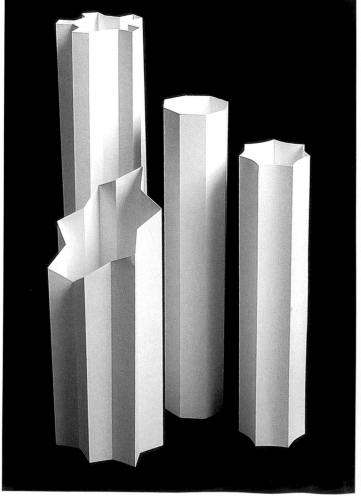

Basic cylinders

Cylinders of different sizes may be used as the body and neck of a full-round figure, as internal spacers in a construction, or as a supporting or decorative column in a design. The simple cylinder is not very strong but may be transformed into a load-bearing structure by scoring and bending.

Basic cylinders are formed by applying bias to a rectangular piece of paper, which gives it an almost cylindrical shape.

Leaving a tab or overlap when cutting to the required size will make it easy to form the completed cylinder. The overlap is then securely glued.

Cones and cylinders can be produced by rolling a biased strip of paper. Cones made in this way would be sharply tapering and suitable for the limbs of a free-standing full-round figure; the cylinders could form the armature or central support for a sculpture.

Decorative forms

Combinations of straight and curved scores can produce a multitude of interesting and decorative forms, ideal for panel and border decoration and display work.

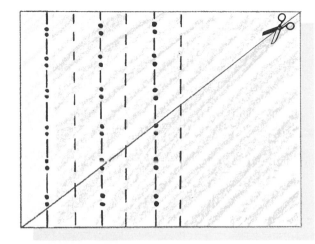

Straight scoring

1 A rectangular piece of paper (say, 30 × 25cm/12 × 10in) is scored alternately on face and reverse sides at 1cm (½in) intervals, as shown. Accurate scoring is the key to the desired effect. The paper is then cut diagonally.

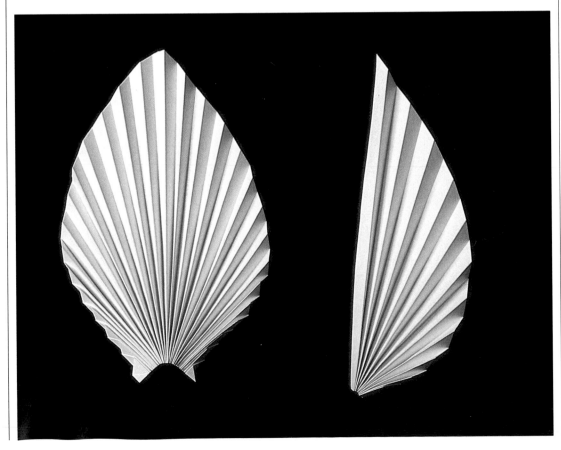

2 Working on a flat surface, apply glue to the base of each pleat at one end only. Then pinch the pleats together to form the shape illustrated. The two shapes obtained from a single piece of paper may be used to produce the leaf effect.

Simple and complex curved scoring

1 As the examples on this page show, many designs may be produced by curved scoring.

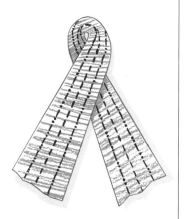

Begin with a U-shape, score, then bend one arm across the other as shown.

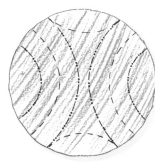
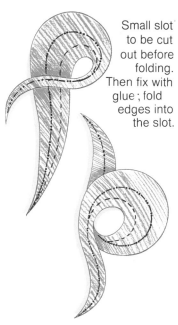

Small slot to be cut out before folding. Then fix with glue ; fold edges into the slot.

Apply glue where the two tails cross over each other to hold the curl in position.

Score a circle like this . . .

. . . or like this. There are many scoring patterns.

Make three scores as shown, to create a cushion-like form.

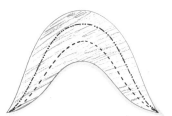

Similar to the crossed-over shapes shown in the first and second columns, this example creates a more open shape.

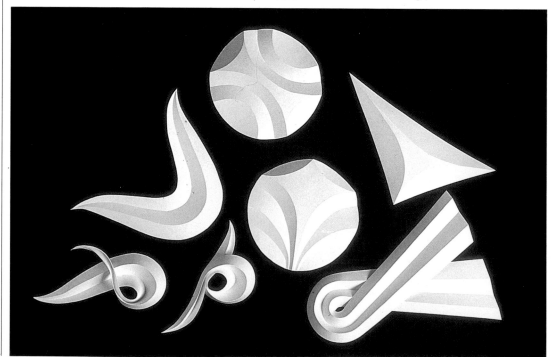

The seven examples diagrammed on this page are here shown photographed. The technique of curved scoring produces forms with movement and expression.

Compound surface scoring

Surface design can be achieved by compound scoring, always on the face side. The simple surface design on the larger example is the result of straight scoring with the paper curved for effect; dimensions are a matter of choice but the marking out needs to be accurate. The photograph shows the same design developed into a cylindrical shape, together with a cylinder using curved scores for its surface design.

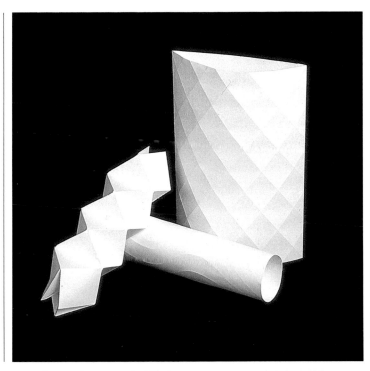

Cut surface treatment

Cutting the surface of the paper at regular intervals will break up a large area and produce interesting effects of light and shade. The technique is particularly useful to convey the impression of feathers, fish scales or petals.

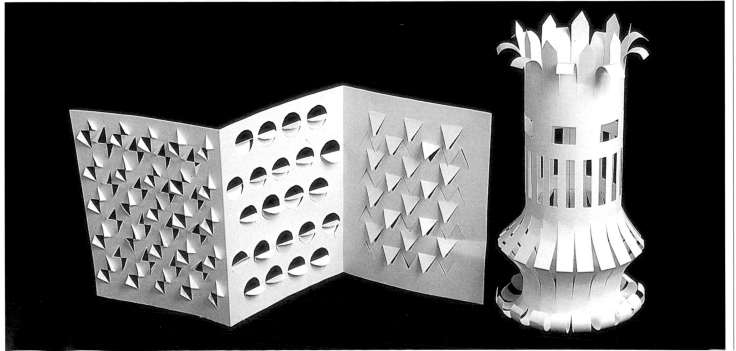

ARMATURES AND ASSEMBLY

The armature is the unseen part of a paper sculpture: its internal supporting structure. Armatures for full-round paper sculptures are quite different from those for half-round or low-relief sculptures.

Full-round

A full-round sculpture needs an internal support that generally follows the shape of the sculpture and enables other components to be built onto it. Materials are a matter of choice, and a medium-sized figure (say, 30cm/12in high) may have as its central support a rolled paper cylinder, a poster tube or a wooden dowel, with suitable cross-pieces for the arms, if necessary. A large structure, on the other hand, may well have an armature constructed of steel strip or wire mesh.

Opposite are various stages in the assembly of an armature for a full-round figure: a chorister.

Half-round and low-relief

The half-round or low-relief sculpture is built up in layers and usually requires a flat armature which both supports the components and keeps the sculpture in shape. The armature has the same profile as the sculpture, but on a slightly smaller scale, so that the sculpture can be attached to it by means of tabs.

For small sculptures card is often adequate, but for large structures the armature may be made of hardboard, plywood or foam sandwich board (polyboard). Do not overlook the possibilities of readily obtainable corrugated cardboard. This has little rigidity but makes a perfectly good armature if two layers are glued together with the corrugations at right angles. The choice of material is vast, but be careful when opting for an armature of flat card. This is liable to warp and it is wise to cover both sides of the card with cartridge paper.

For many half-round sculptures the armature itself is built up in sections with suitable spacers, such as rolled paper coils, giving the effect of depth to the completed work. The dragon on page 182 is a large sculpture with a cross corrugated cardboard armature for the body and an armature built up to give depth.

Assembly

Sometimes Sellotape, double-sided tape or an unseen staple may be all that is needed. But for most fastenings, use a good quality glue, such as UHU, that is quick-drying but allows you sufficient time to change your mind. PVA adhesives need to be used with care as they can cause distortion of the paper; they are best used, undiluted, on heavier papers or in minute quantities on small items.

Mirror tile fixing pads are useful when mounting a half-round or low-relief sculpture for display, and enable easy removal of the sculpture by slicing through the pad.

Tabbing methods

The fixing of one component to another, or the fixing of a half-round sculpture to its armature, is frequently done by means of tabs. There are two types of tab:
• Integral tabs These are cut as part of the component, scored and bent back if necessary, and glued.
• Separate tabs These are made by cutting suitable lengths from a strip of paper, scoring and bending, and positioning just inside the edge of the component to be attached. This method leaves the component with a smooth unbroken contour, so that separate tabs are generally preferable to integral tabs when the contours are visible.

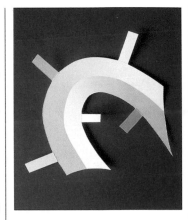

Integral tabs
The tabs can be seen cut from the same sheet as the U-shaped component.

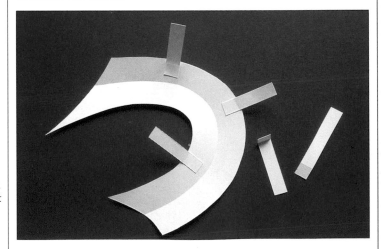

Separate tabs
Here, the tabs are made separately and fastened to the component.

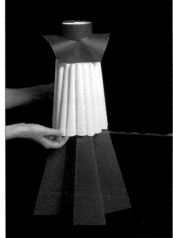

Full-round armature
1 Glue the flange to the main support. Glue the front and rear edges of the flange to the support.

3 Add the top surplice, making sure the pleats fall neatly.

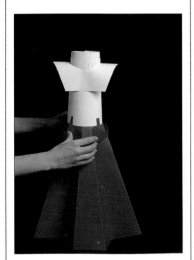

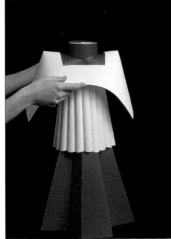

2 Fix the skirt to the main support, using the tabs. It may help to gather the pleats if a belt is added. Make sure that the box pleat is to the front.

4 Add the surplice, resting it on the flange. The armature is now complete. Separately made head and arm units may now be added.

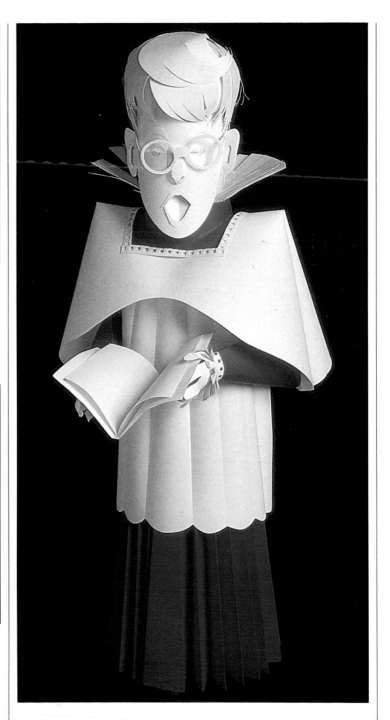

5 The completed sculpture of a chorister.

Half-round and low-relief armature

1 The armature for the sculpture of a leopard in which the head is half round and the body is low relief. The piece is made in 1mm mount board covered both sides with cartridge paper.

2 The armature with some components fitted. One leg is reversed to illustrate fitting by tabs.

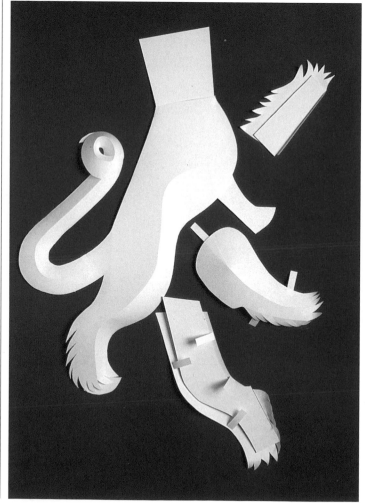

3 The completed sculpture. The rear fore and hind legs are spaced away from the back of the main body armature by means of rolled paper coils.

DAVID COOK
Coat of arms

Commissioned by a Town Council, the piece is in low relief. Interest is given to an otherwise uniform surface by the careful use of textured papers (see detail right), all from the same manufactured range. Note the precise cutting of the paper shapes and the subtle shadows beneath them. The paper sculpting element here is minimal: perhaps a better technical description would be "paper layering". Height: 45cm (20in)

MADS KRABBE
Music

The piece was designed specifically to be photographed, whereas the Coat of arms (left) was designed to be seen as a model. The delicate curved scoring of the shapes laid over the frame and the low angle of lighting combined to create a strong photographic image. The violin and figures are made in a very much more subtle manner – the violin in particular being beautifully crafted. (Student project: Coventry Polytechnic). Height: 40cm (18in)

This low-relief sculpture of an owl in flight shows how the techniques described in the preceding pages build into a finished design that you can make.

The owl has a wing span of 40cm (16in) and a height of 42cm (nearly 17in). When completed, it should be spaced slightly away from the surface of a display board to give a three-dimensional effect.

With the exception of the armatures (which are made in thin card), all the pieces can be made in cartridge paper. Body unit 1 and the feather unit are cut, with the grain, from paper to which bias has been applied. All scoring is on the face side except where indicated on the tail unit. Feather effects are cut and raised and edges are fringed to the approximate depth indicated on the patterns. The patterns are illustrated approximately one third full size but may be scaled up to any required size.

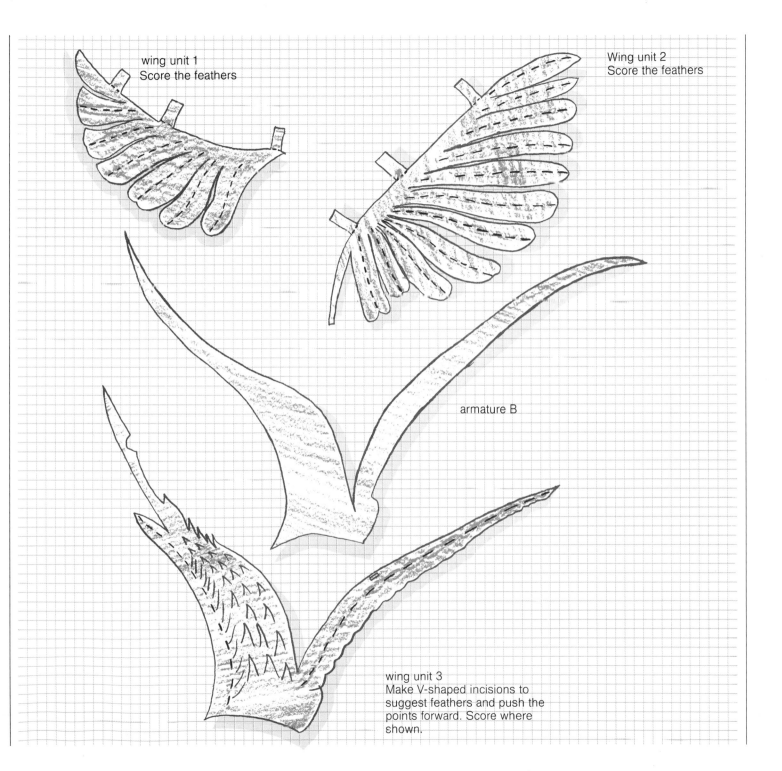

wing unit 1
Score the feathers

Wing unit 2
Score the feathers

armature B

wing unit 3
Make V-shaped incisions to
suggest feathers and push the
points forward. Score where
shown.

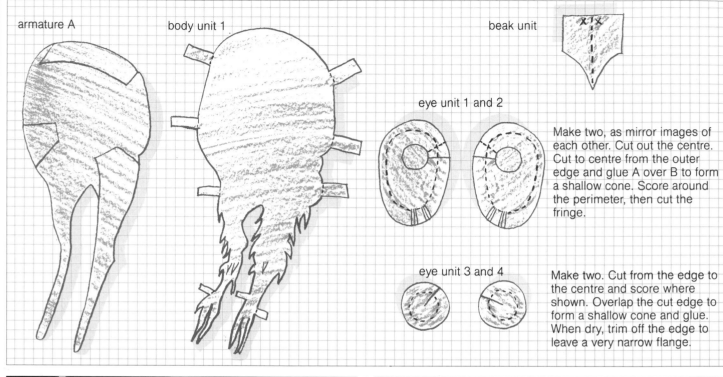

armature A

body unit 1

beak unit

eye unit 1 and 2

Make two, as mirror images of each other. Cut out the centre. Cut to centre from the outer edge and glue A over B to form a shallow cone. Score around the perimeter, then cut the fringe.

eye unit 3 and 4

Make two. Cut from the edge to the centre and score where shown. Overlap the cut edge to form a shallow cone and glue. When dry, trim off the edge to leave a very narrow flange.

Assembly

1 Glue armature A to armature B.

2 Attach wing units 1 and 2, using the tabs. Glue the narrow strip at the bottom of unit 2 to the armature. Attach body unit 1 to the armature, using the tabs. The unit is wider than the armature, so must be curved forward to become narrower.

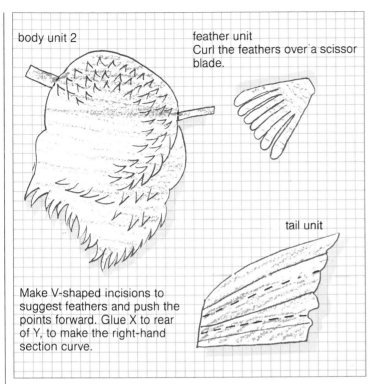

body unit 2

feather unit
Curl the feathers over a scissor blade.

tail unit

Make V-shaped incisions to suggest feathers and push the points forward. Glue X to rear of Y, to make the right-hand section curve.

4 Glue eye units 3 and 4 into units 1 and 2. Glue one half of the face to each side of the beak unit. Attach tabs to the back of each pupil and use them to attach the face to body unit 2.

3 Attach wing unit 3 over the top of units 1 and 2, using the tabs. Glue the tip of 3 to 2. Glue the base of 3 to the base of the wing armature. Attach body unit 2 to body unit 1, slightly higher at the left than at the right, to accentuate the illusion of a solid body thrusting forward.

5 Attach tail and feather units to back of armature 1. Nightflight complete. Note how careful layering, shaping and scoring can create a convincing illusion of depth and volume, even though the sculpture is in very low relief.

PAPIER-MÂCHÉ

CASTING FROM A MOLD

USING OTHER MOLDS

Papier-mâché is a French term meaning "mashed paper." It was first coined, not in France but in eighteenth-century London, by French émigré workers who made papier-mâché objects in small workshops. Only recently have the French themselves recognized the term.

In recent years, papier-mâché has undergone a major revival. Its versatility and low-tech method make it an ideal medium for the craftsperson with little space or few facilities.

Torn paper strips
Layering strips of torn paper is the more common of the two papier-mâché techniques. It is used to cast from a mold, or former, and involves building up many layers of pasted paper. Although basically a very simple process, it needs to be worked with great care to get a good finish.

When you use a mold – for example, an existing bowl – it must be well prepared by coating with a layer of releasing agent, such as Vaseline or soft soap. This will prevent the first layer of paper from sticking to the mold. It is important to build up the layers of paper, taking care to smooth each piece down with the fingers so that no air or lumps of paste are trapped between the layers of paper to disfigure the final piece when it is dry.

Equipment and materials
Newsprint is very flexible and adaptable when soaked with paste or glue. The paper must be torn – not cut – into strips along the grain of the newspaper, generally down the columns of type. The slight roughness of the edges produces smoother and less obvious joins when they are pasted down than you can get with cut edges.

If possible, it is a good idea to use two different colored newspapers, as this makes the counting of the layers easier. Lay the paper in one direction for one layer, then crosswise for the next. This gives the piece more strength.

When casting from a more complicated form, it is better to use smaller, thinner pieces of newspaper. These will mold themselves to the form without creasing because of their ability to stretch around a curved surface.

An interesting variation would be to layer with different kinds of paper. Fewer layers would be necessary if you use thicker, handmade papers (see PAPERMAKING), although they would need to be torn into smaller pieces to cover a curved surface without creasing. A piece layered in this way need not be painted.

Colored or dyed paper can be used, thus enhancing and revealing the technique of layering, while integrating the decoration of the piece with its construction. Tissue paper will produce a delicate but fragile piece.

The use of different kinds and strengths of paper – making a collage in three dimensions, in fact – is an exciting and worthwhile way to explore the many possibilities of layering.

Adhesives
It is equally possible to use a cellulose paste (wallpaper paste) or white glue. The cellulose is more comfortable to work with, though great care must be taken when using pastes that contain fungicide. White glue is very sticky to work with, but will produce a strong finished piece. As a compromise, it is possible to mix the two glues: the consistency should be that of heavy cream. The use of glue or paste is a matter of individual preference, and it is advisable to try both methods.

The glue or paste should be spread onto each side of the strip of paper separately. The paste must be allowed to soak through the paper to render it

more flexible, but it should not be wet. It is an idea to paste up a few pieces at a time and lay them around the edge of the paste bowl, ready for use. They will soon dry, and so must be used quickly. Alternatively, a larger piece of paper may be pasted, and strips torn from it to be applied to the mold.

Applying the layers
The number of layers put on obviously depends on the required thickness of the finished article. About ten would be enough for a bowl, as this would be further strengthened by the use of lacquer, paint and varnish. About eight layers would be enough for a mask.

It is possible to add all the layers in one go, but allowing each layer to dry before applying the next may produce a more reliable and smoother finish, particularly when using cellulose paste. This is a matter of personal preference. There are no absolute rules when using papier-mâché, and each

artist discovers and refines her or his own techniques.

Drying
Drying times vary according to the working environment. It is always best to let the piece dry at an even temperature – a warm place is ideal. Drying may be speeded by putting the piece in the oven on a very low temperature. Rapid drying may cause distortion and would be unwise when casting from a modeling clay mold, because the clay would degenerate.

When the object is dry, release the cast and finish the object.

Finishing
In the case of a bowl, the uneven rim may be trimmed to make a neat edge. Any cut edges should be bound with two layers of pasted paper.

There are many alternative and imaginative ways to treat the rim, which will influence the form and character of the bowl. For example, when layering, allow the torn paper

to stick out from the mold and, when thoroughly dry, tear into a ragged edge. The rim may be cut unevenly, scalloped or zigzagged, or cut through like a lattice. Other possibilities would be to add paper or cardboard to the rim. PULP may be added to form a softer or more sculpted rim. If the papier-mâché is cut, however, always remember to add two layers to cover the cut.

The form may also be altered by the addition of a foot at the bottom of the bowl, but always cover any introduced material with two layers of paper to unify the whole.

For ideas on decoration, see below.

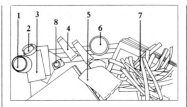

Equipment checklist
1 lacquer for sealing (optional)
2 Vaseline
3 selection of papers for creating different effects (optional)
4 acrylic paints for decoration (optional)
5 wallpaper paste
6 plastic glue
7 newspapers torn into strips
8 varnish

CASTING FROM A MOULD

It is possible to cast from a range of moulds but it's probably easiest to start with a bowl. To get a good finish the layers need to be worked with care – so don't rush.

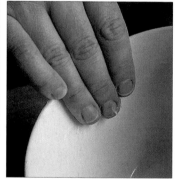

1 In this example, the mould is a bowl – an easy shape to cast from. Cover it with a releasing agent, such as Vaseline or soft soap. Take care to include the inside and top of the rim.

2 Tear the newspaper down the grain in strips 4cm (1½in) wide. Tear again into 8cm (3in) lengths.

3 Use a wide bowl to mix the paste in, and paste each piece of paper separately with the fingers. Ensure the strips are not soaked and that there are no lumps of paste attached.

4 Lay the strips of paper into the mould, smoothing each piece separately and overlapping each one until the first layer is complete.

5 Lay the second layer of paper over the first, crosswise for strength. Use a paper of a different colour for each layer (eg white and pink newspaper). Cover very evenly. Continue with alternating colours until ten layers are finished. Smooth each layer to eliminate any bubbles.

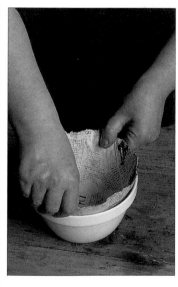

6 When completely dry, ease the top of the cast away from the mould.

7 Then twist, and the cast bowl will release. If there is any reluctance, or if the first layer seems damp, allow to dry for a little longer.

8 The rim can be cut evenly with a scalpel, if a smooth, neat finish is required.

9 Finally, add two layers of pasted paper to disguise the sharp cut edge of the bowl.

Adding a paper rim
1 Cut the rim evenly with a scalpel.

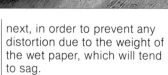

2 Add pasted paper strips to the edge of the rim. Allow each layer to dry before applying the next, in order to prevent any distortion due to the weight of the wet paper, which will tend to sag.

3 Add six layers.

4 Cut the extended rim to shape and cover the cut with two layers of pasted paper.

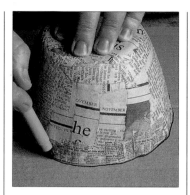

Adding a cardboard rim
1 After the rim of the bowl has been evenly cut, turn the bowl upside down on a piece of thin cardboard and trace the circumference onto it.

2 Cut the centre out of the card, then cut around the outer edge to form a ring.

3 Fit the rim onto the bowl. Attach the rim with white glue.

4 Secure with masking tape until dry.

5 Remove the tape, then cover the two surfaces of the rim and the join to the bowl with two layers of pasted paper.

YANINA TEMPLE
Dish
The dish has been made by layering paper over a mold.
Diameter: 14in (36cm)

It is possible to make one-piece casts from a huge range of objects, as long as they are not complicated shapes. For example:
- balls
- balloons
- plates
- flowerpots
- woks

Always cast from the inside of a bowl or flowerpot in order to release the paper cast in one piece. There is a certain amount of shrinkage of the paper during the drying process, which makes it difficult to release the cast from the outer surface of this kind of mold.

Multipiece molds

Vases and pitchers can be used as molds, but the paper must be cut in order to release it from the mold, and then re-joined afterwards.

Such is the versatility of the technique that casts can be taken from anything, from apples to dolls. The more complicated the form, the smaller the pieces of paper should be, in order to cover a variety of curved surfaces without creasing.

When dry, the cast must be cut from the form in two halves with a scalpel. The sections should be released like the two halves of a shell. They must then be glued back together with a small quantity of strong glue. Hold the halves together temporarily with masking tape while the glue dries. The join should then be disguised with two layers of pasted paper torn into thin strips.

Layering a self-made mold

Another approach to the layering method is to construct a mold yourself. This alternative offers numerous possibilities. The simplest, perhaps, is a traditional relief mask (demonstrated below), but it is entirely possible to make three-dimensional objects, where the paper is layered on all sides of the mold.

Although modeling clay is a suitable material for making a mold, the form to be cast can be made from a variety of materials, depending on size. The most important consideration is that the paper can be easily released from the mold.

The methods for three materials are described here: modeling clay, (with step-by-step instructions), plaster of Paris and wire.

How to make a plaster mold

A more permanent mold for a mask or a relief form can be made from plaster of Paris. Model the form in clay; then build a retaining wall with wooden boards or clay 1in/2cm higher than the mold. The whole structure should be built on a wooden board and the walls sealed to the board to prevent seepage. Mix the plaster according to the instructions, until it becomes creamy. Pour this mixture gently into the mold until it reaches the top of the retaining wall. Tap the work surface to force out any bubbles trapped inside. The plaster warms as it sets. When set, turn over and remove the clay. Allow the mold to dry thoroughly; then coat with shellac to seal the surface. The plaster mold is a negative. Proceed with the torn paper technique as described on the previous pages, or the PULP technique.

How to make a mold over a wire armature

To make a larger, free-standing piece, it will be necessary to layer the papier-mâché over a wire armature. Use a block of wood as a base and build an armature from aluminum wire or chicken wire. Create a modeling clay form around this armature and proceed with the torn-paper technique as before, remembering to coat the mold first with a releasing agent. When all the layers have been applied and have thoroughly dried, cut the cast from the mold and reassemble as described for multipiece molds. There will be a hole at the bottom of the cast where the wire armature was attached to the wooden base. This can easily be covered by a few layers of paper.

How to make a clay mold
1 Model the shape of the mask on a wooden board. Take care not to allow any part to stick out too far, as this will cause difficulties when releasing the mask.

2 Coat the mold with an even layer of Vaseline or soft soap.

3 Apply the first layer of paper, using very small pieces. Carefully smooth the paper to remove air bubbles and excess paste.

4 Cover with eight layers in alternate colours. Allow to dry very thoroughly before removing from the mould.

7 Cover the cut edges of the mask with two layers of paper. Allow to dry thoroughly before painting.

5 Release the cast by prising the edges away from the Plasticine with fingers or a blunt knife.

6 Trim the uneven edge of the mask, so that it can lie level.

MIKE CHASE
Mask
The piece is made inside a negative plaster mould, taken from an original clay positive. The papier mâché is layered, allowed to dry and any blemishes filled in with modelling paste. Finally, the surface is painted with acrylic. The mask is not decorative, but was made specifically for an actor adopting the persona of a defensive character.
Lifesize

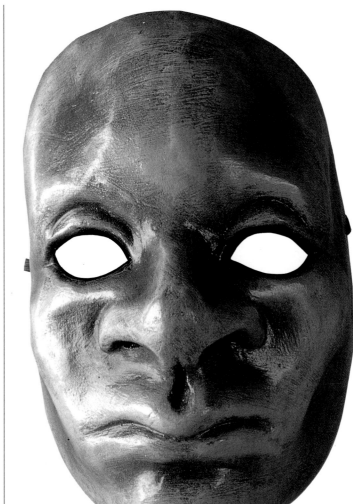

PULPING

CARDBOARD MOULDS

An alternative to the PAPIER MÂCHÉ layering method is to make up a paper pulp. This can then be pressed into, or shaped over, any of the moulds discussed under papier mâché. It is a much quicker method for building up thickness than layering. Patterns and decoration can be created by using impressions from textured objects. The pulp can also be formed on its own without a mould.

JUDITH FAERBER
Untitled
The piece is made by placing differently coloured pulps onto a flat bed of white pulp (for added strength). The mushy pulp is flattened under a heavy press, which compresses the fibres and squeezes out the water. 48×48cm (19×19in)

Equipment and materials

Try to find shredded paper. Otherwise, any of the papers suggested for the papier-mâché torn-paper method will work. Tear the paper into ½in (1cm) squares.

Equipment checklist
1 kitchen blender or electric whisk
2 plaster of Paris (or cellulose filler)
3 linseed oil; a few spoonfuls help make pulp workable
4 white glue (and/or wallpaper paste containing fungicide)
5 oil of cloves, a few drops to help prevent mold
6 shredded paper
7 large saucepan (preferably one not used for cooking)
8 strainer (or colander)

How to make the pulp
1 Soak a large saucepanful of shredded or torn paper in water overnight.

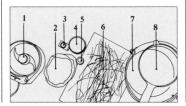

2 Simmer the soaked paper over low heat for 20 minutes.

3 If the paper has not been finely shredded, blend or whisk the paper mix to help break it down.

4 Strain the mixture through a strainer or colander. Lightly squeeze out excess water, but be careful not to condense the pulp to a hard, waterless mass.

5 Thoroughly mix in 1 cup of glue.

6 Sprinkle in enough dry wallpaper paste to give the pulp a workable consistency, mixing it quickly. Fillers and oil can be added if necessary.

7 Store the pulp in a plastic bag in the refrigerator or use immediately.

Using pulp to make a plate
1 Line the top of the plate mould with cling film.

2 Press the paper pulp evenly onto the inside of the plate mould to a thickness of about 7-14mm (¼-½in). Leave to dry slightly.

3 Smooth the surface of the pulp with the back of a metal spoon.

4 Decorate the rim with more pulp, then leave to dry in a warm place.

5 Remove the pulp plate from the mould. Finish the underside by making a foot-rim with more pulp.

6 When the pulp is completely dry, seal it with a coat of gesso or a 1:3 mixture of PVA and acrylic paint.

CARDBOARD MOULDS

An easy way to make large pieces is to start with a cardboard base, build up bulk with newspaper, then cover this base structure with a thin layer of paper pulp. By building in this way, less pulp is used and it dries faster and more evenly. The cardboard structure gives the piece its strength – not the pulp – so it is important to attach handles or other additions very firmly *before* the pulp is added.

Any type of card can be used to make the base: corrugated cardboard, mounting card, cartons, carpet rolls, card tubes, polyboard (a sandwich of foam and card), etc. To make a strong enough base, use polyboard or laminate several layers of cardboard held together with PVA. For mirror frames, remember to cover the glass with masking tape to protect the surface from pulp and glue.

Making a tray
1 Cut out all the shapes needed for the base, handles, etc.

2 Attach the handles firmly to the base, using staples, tape, and any other means to ensure a solid structure.

3 To build up the rim, use scrunched up newspaper, glued and taped into place.

7 If desired, finish the underside of the tray by gluing on a backing, such as textured wallpaper or felt.

8 When the tray is completely dry, brush on a coat of lacquer or a 1:3 mixture of glue and acrylic paint. This will seal the surface prior to decorating.

4 Brush on glue and mold the pulp firmly into place over the rim and handles.

5 Decorate the rim with, say, molded pulp. Allow to dry slightly until the pulp is firm.

6 Turn the tray over and add more pulp to the underside of the rim and handles to strengthen them.

9 The finished tray.

DECORATIVE IDEAS FOR PAPIER MÂCHÉ AND PAPER PULP

Ideas for decorating PAPIER MÂCHÉ and PAPER PULP are endless. Illustrations of fine decorative finishes may provide inspiration, but there are no set rules, and decoration is up to your own imagination. If collage has been used as part of the layering technique, of course, further decoration is unnecessary.

Interesting decorative effects may be achieved by adding objects to form a relief pattern, either under the top layer of the layer method, or on top of it but under the primer layer of paint. String can provide free-flowing embossed lines. Seeds, shells and pieces of card may be used, stuck down with PVA.

DECOUPAGE techniques may be used to decorate the surface, perhaps combined with painting, and heavily varnished to create the traditional decoupage, glassy effect.

The application of precious-metal leaf is a surprisingly uncomplicated process, which will magically transform papier mâché. The metal leaf enhances the textured surface of the paper and cleverly belies its humble origin.

It is necessary to prime the papier mâché surface before decorating it. This will prevent the paint from being absorbed by the porous paper. Acrylic primer will make a good, matt white surface to work on.

A more interesting surface can be obtained with the use of traditional gesso, which is made from rabbit-skin size, soaked overnight in water. This is heated in a double saucepan with ground chalk and whisked to the consistency of single cream. It is applied hot, in several layers, and dries very hard, so strengthening the

piece and giving it a finish that resembles porcelain. The gesso itself may be coloured with powder paint. An ancient-looking mottled effect can be created by painting colour layer by layer over the gesso, sanding each layer as it dries.

Painted patterns may be applied, but always with sensitive references to the form. Acrylic or gouache (water-based) paints are ideal. Try to paint directly onto the surface of the papier mâché. Use bold, confident strokes.

Sealing

Before priming, it is possible to go some way towards waterproofing papier mâché by coating it with three or four layers of linseed oil. It should then be baked at a low temperature until completely dry.

Varnishes

A variety of finishes are gained through the use of different varnishes. Many layers of polyurethane varnish, sanded lightly between each coat, will

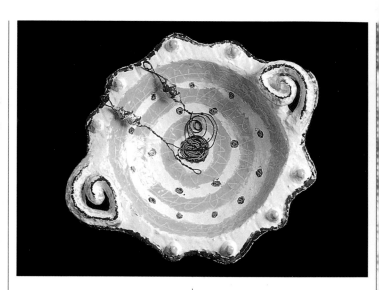

MADELEINE CHILD
Bowls
▲ ▶ These pieces are made using the PAPER PULP technique over a mould, with the handles being made from cardboard covered with pulp. The surface decoration is achieved with acrylic paint sealed with varnish.
Diameter: 40cm (16in)

produce a glassy effect. However, the varnish has the disadvantage of yellowing with age. A single coat of matt varnish will seal a painted surface but will not be obviously visible.

Pigments may be added to varnish. This will give an ageing effect when applied over painted or collaged decoration.

Papier mâché objects treated with varnish will never be completely waterproof and must not be expected to hold liquids. They can, however, be wiped clean with a damp cloth without damage.

MELINDA WHILE
Bowls
▲ These bowls are made by layering newspaper over a mold. The final layer is layout paper, crumpled up and dipped in tea to give a little color to the surface. The motifs are lino prints made on a flat sheet of tea-stained paper, then cut out and glued to the surface of the bowls. A matte varnish finish is applied from an aerosol.
Diameters: approx 10in (25cm)

JACQUELINE SHELTON
Bowl
► Made by the conventional layering technique, the surface is decorated with oil pastel. The large shells are not only a decorative motif, but become part of the form of the bowl.
Height: 6in (15cm)

CAROLYN QUARTERMAINE
Plaque
▲ The body of the plaque is made by layering newspaper over a mold. Onto this, layers of colored silk are applied, silk-screened with calligraphic motifs. Note the use of color to balance the composition and create focal points for the eye. The artist's plaques form part of a larger body of non-paper designs, both practical and decorative.
Diameter: 18in (46cm)

CAROLYN QUARTERMAINE
Plaque
◄ This piece is made in the same way as the one above. Both are affixed to the wall by means of a short length of cord, the ends of which are embedded into the back of the plaque beneath layers of papier-mâché.
Diameter: 22in (56cm)

JACQUELINE SHELTON
Bowl and urn

◄ The widest part of the urn is layered as a band around any mould of the appropriate diameter. When dry, the band is removed from the mould, then the top half of the urn is made from paper strips that coil around and around upwards from the band, much as a coiled ceramic pot is made. Thus, the shape is built freehand without a mould. The top half is allowed to dry, then the lower half is built downwards in a similar manner. When dry, the surface is painted white, then covered with oil pastels thinned with turpentine and rubbed until a patina appears. Over this, pulp, shells, glass, stones, gold powder and other materials are added. Finally, the surface is sealed. The bowl is made in a similar way.
Height of urn: (16in); bowl: (7in)

JACQUELINE SHELTON
Urn

▲ The piece is made in the same way as the pieces on the left. Note the wonderfully sumptuous surface achieved by the artist's decorative technique, complemented by the asymmetry of the form.
Height: 43cm (17in)

JACQUELINE SHELTON
Urns

► Made as described above, these near-identical pieces show how the hand-built technique and surface decoration effectively achieve a quality of individuality from an otherwise repetitious process.
Height: 12.5cm (5in)

CAROLINE GIBBS
Bowl

▼ The basic structure of the bowls on this page is made conventionally by layering PAPIER MÂCHÉ over a mould. The surface is then gessoed and covered with several layers of a mixture of finely ground clay mixed with glue, later carefully sanded. This now smooth surface is dampened and metal leaf applied to create the beaten metal finish. Silver leaf is often oxidized with ammonia hydrosulphide and sealed. Gold leaf requires no seal, except a waterproofing agent.
Diameter: 30cm (12in)

CAROLINE GIBBS
Bowls

▲ Made as described to the left, the three bowls on this page are examples of a continuing series of work that explores metalized finishes applied to PAPIER MÂCHÉ forms. The appearance is very much that of a bowl made from beaten metal – the paper interior is almost incidental.
Diameter: approximately 20cm (8in)

PAPER MAKING

For most of its 2,000-year history, paper has been made by hand. Only since the Industrial Revolution has the process become mechanized. The technology of modern papermaking is very complex, yet the basic process remains so simple that even a child can make paper.

Papermaking is spontaneous, open-ended and decorative, and it is also highly satisfying. A little time must be spent beforehand to prepare molds and deckles and to assemble equipment, but once everything is organized, paper can be made time and again.

Equipment and materials
We waste an enormous amount of paper, much of which could be recycled, such as photocopy, computer or typing paper, and

many more. It is worth approaching local printers, colleges and offices who might be able to provide good quality offcuts and would be pleased to see their waste going to good use.

Avoid using paper that has a lot of black type on it: the plainer the better. Newspaper, being highly acidic, will turn yellow and brittle too quickly. Slick magazines should also be avoided. If in doubt, test a small amount to see if it gives the desired result. The following pages show you how to make a sheet of paper very simply (by the Western method). Handmade paper made by skilled papermakers uses practically the same method, the only difference being the quality of materials and equipment.

Paper should be presoaked, preferably overnight or a couple of hours beforehand.

You will need:
• paper, presoaked overnight or a couple of hours beforehand.
• plastic sheets. Papermaking is a wet business, so all surfaces will need to be covered, including yourself.
• plastic tub should be large enough to accommodate the mold and deckle with your hands on both sides.
• kitchen blender (1 quart/liter capacity).
• boards (approximately 13×15in/32×32cm) should be rigid and nonabsorbent; if wood is used, prime it first. Two boards are needed.
• net curtain material should have a close enough weave to

prevent pulp from escaping.
• interfacing or Vilene is an excellent support material for freshly made sheets. It is available from the dressmaking department of large stores. Buy 4yd (4m) of the sew-in variety, medium-weight; the iron-on type has undesirable chemicals in it. Less expensive and good for beginners are handiwipes or nonwoven household cleaning cloths, but these do contain chemicals that may eventually harm your paper. It is also important not to choose a material with too much texture as this will imprint itself on your sheets. Cut the material into 10½×13in (26×32cm) pieces.
• felts. A local secondhand shop will usually have a supply of old wool blankets, which make a perfect substitute for the felts used in papermaking mills. They should be cut into 12×14in (30×35cm) pieces.
• mold and deckle, bought or made.

Optional extras
Additional items include: Formica (as a surface to dry sheets on). A 3in (8cm) paint brush (only needed if transferring damp sheets to a board for drying).

Care of equipment
Wash interfacings after use and hang up to dry. The felts should also be hung up to dry. Rinse off the mold and deckle at the end of a session. Keep everything as clean as possible and in a dry place.

Storing pulp
Pulp can be stored for a few days, but it will eventually start to rot and smell. To store the pulp temporarily, strain it through a strainer and netting. Keep it in an airtight container. A preservative (oil of cloves or thymol) can be added to give it a slightly longer life.

Alternatively, squeeze out as much water as possible from the pulp while it is in the netting, then lay it out to dry naturally. Once dry, store it in plastic bags and reuse when needed. Never pour pulp mixture down the kitchen sink; it will cause a blockage.

Equipment checklist
1 net curtain material
2 wool blankets (or felts)
3 mold and deckle
4 plastic sheets
5 boards
6 interfacing or Vilene
7 plastic tub
8 paintbrush
9 kitchen blender

MAKING A MOULD AND DECKLE

A mould and deckle is the piece of equipment used for actually forming a sheet of paper. The mould is a frame with mesh stretched over it; the deckle is the frame that fits on top. A mould and deckle can be bought from a craft shop or you can make your own. You will need:

- 1.70m (68in) length of 21mm (³/₄in) square wood
- curtain netting or nylon/metal mesh
- staple gun or drawing pins (avoid materials that rust)
- L-shaped brass plates with screws less deep than the wood
- screwdriver
- scissors
- saw
- polyurethane varnish
- wood glue
- insulating tape
- draught excluder tape
- sandpaper

1 The best wood to use is a hardwood, such as mahogany. Cut the wood into four 20cm (8in) lengths and four 22.5cm (9in) lengths. Place them together to make two separate frames of identical size. Glue the corners and screw the brass plates at each corner on one side. If you have the tools and skill, it is a good idea to make more secure mitred or lap joints, using wood glue and screws. Sandpaper any sharp edges. Varnishing the wood will make it tougher.

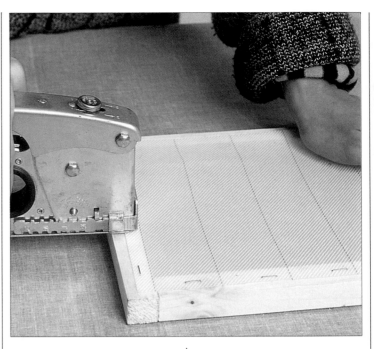

2 The mesh has to be stretched tensely and evenly over one frame to make the mould. Place the mesh over the frame (on the opposite side from the brass plates), leaving at least 21mm (³/₄in) overhang. Stiff mesh should be cut to the right size before stretching. Staple from the middle of each side and work outwards to the corners.

3 Trim the mesh in line with the outside edge or just within it. Then place tape over mesh and wood to seal untidy fraying or sharp edges.

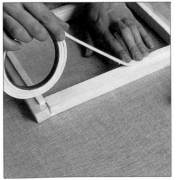

4 The deckle – the other identical frame – is made exactly like the mould without the mesh. Draught excluder tape placed along the edge of the deckle that will be placed together with the mould will help the mould and deckle fit snugly.

MAKING PULP

Ideally the paper to be used for recycling should be soaked overnight, having first been torn into 5cm (2in) squares. Using a paper shredder is a big time saver.

1 Fill the blender no more than three-quarters full with warm water, then take a small fistful of paper and blend. The blender should not be overstrained. If it sounds overloaded, take out some pulp and top up with water. Short bursts on the blender are best to prevent the motor from burning out. For soft paper, a 10-second run should be sufficient. Use several bursts for tougher paper.

2 Pour the pulp into a clean tub. Carry on pulping and filling until the tub is half full. Then top up to three-quarters full with warm water.

MAKING PAPER

The pulp and water mixture in the tub needs to be stirred gently before starting a new sheet, as pulp tends to settle at the bottom. Try to develop the steps listed below into a smooth, continuous action.

2 Hold the two firmly together with the deckle on top. Move hands to the back edge of the tub, holding the mold and deckle vertically, and with arms outstretched. Dip the mold and deckle into tub and scoop up the pulp by quickly moving the mold and deckle toward the body and simultaneously changing to a horizontal angle.

3 Lift the mold and deckle out of the mixture and let the water drain back into the tub. Gently shake the mold and deckle from side to side and back and forth to distribute the fibers of the pulp evenly.

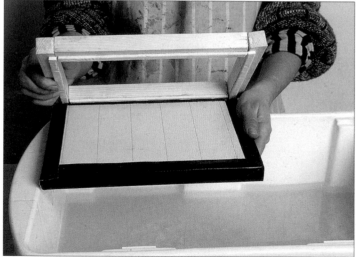

1 Place deckle (taped edge downward) on top of the mold.

4 When most of the water has drained back into the tub, continue draining by tipping from one corner.

5 After a few seconds, rest the mold and deckle on the edge of the tub and carefully remove the deckle without dripping onto your freshly made sheet. The sheet is ready for the next stage, couching. If the sheet is unsatisfactory, place the mold face down on the surface of the mixture in the tub and start again.

Couching

Couching is the action of transferring the wet layer of pulp on the mould to the support material (interfacing or cloth). Underneath the interfacing should be placed one layer of cut up blanket and beneath this a board. Wet both the interfacing and the blanket, as this greatly helps the couching process. Place them directly one beneath the other, ensuring that there are no creases. Steps 1, 2 and 3 should be done in a continuous, firm movement.

You may find when couching that the pulp refuses to come off the mould. This could be because the sheet is too thin, in which case you need to put more pulp in the tub. Alternatively the sheet might be too dry. Gently rewet it by placing the mould flat, pulp side up, just touching the surface of the water. This allows the pulp to soak up more water. Then try couching again.

The felt and support material might also be too dry, or you may not be exerting enough pressure during the couching action. It can help to use fingers to press down the back of the mould while it is flat on the supporting material.

1 With the longest edge of the mould vertically in front, place the freshly drained mould on the right side of the support material.

2 Firmly lower the upper edge of the mould. The sheet should be pulp face down in the middle of the support material.

3 Raise the right side of the mould with the right hand and then remove the left edge of the mould. The wet sheet is now resting centrally on the support material.

4 To carry on making more sheets, simply cover the first one with a piece of interfacing placed centrally on top. Place the next sheet to lie on top of the one below. If you have plenty of blanket pieces, place them between interfacings to soak up the water. The pile, or post as it is known in the trade, can consist of as many as 12 to 15 sheets or just one. Complete the pile with a blanket topped by the second board. It is now ready for pressing.

PRESSING, DRYING SIZING

The more water that is pressed out the better. There are several ways of doing this. The one described on this page is the most basic. Take the pile of papers with the boards at either end. Place some newspaper on top of this. Now go to an area where wetness doesn't matter, like the garden. Step onto the pile and move gently around to press all areas. Grab a few more people for extra weight.

Drying
There are two main ways of drying: firstly on boards of Formica, perspex or wood (be careful that the wood does not stain the paper), see right.

The second method of drying is air drying. Simply separate the interfacings with the damp papers on them and lay them out to dry, one beside the other on a clean, flat surface like a carpet. This is very space-consuming. Alternatively, remove the sheets onto dry interfacing or a sheet of bought paper. This is done by placing the interfacing with the wet sheet face down onto the dry interfacing and pressing firmly with the back of the hand. Then gently peel back the wet interfacing, leaving the paper transferred.

Gently remove paper when thoroughly dry.

Sizing
Once the paper is dry, it will be as absorbent as blotting paper. This is called "waterleaf" paper. In order for the paper to have the necessary strength, say for painting, calligraphy or printing, it will have to be sized. The amount of size added will vary according to intended use: writing paper needs to be more heavily sized than water-colour paper, for example.

There are two ways to size:
● Starch sizing. Simply add a tablespoonful of laundry starch to your tub and follow directions on the packet.
● Gelatine sizing. You will need a tray, 5cm (2in) deep, cooking gelatine and blotting paper.

Pressing
The key to this technique is to ensure that as much water as possible is squeezed out. Find an area where wetness doesn't matter, such as the garden. Take the pile of papers with the boards at either end. Place newspaper on top of this. Step onto the pile and move gently around to press all areas.

Sizing
1 Dissolve 1tsp of gelatine in a cup of boiled water, add to tray and top up with warm water till 2.5cm (1in) deep. Place one sheet in the tray and it will absorb the gelatine liquid.

Place one hand, with fingers spread, underneath the sheet, then lift it out and drain it from one corner. Place the sheet on blotting paper to dry.

Board drying
1 After pressing, take off the top board and felt. Carefully pick up the first interfacing with the damp paper on it.

3 With a brush, firmly brush the back of the interfacing and paper, using both horizontal and vertical strokes.

4 Carefully peel off the interfacing, leaving the paper on the board. Double check that all sides are flat on the board; if not, gently press with fingertips.

2 Place this interfacing paper face down on a clean board and press gently down.

MAKING PULP FROM FIBRES

Papers made from fibres contain beautiful effects. A wonderful sense of achievement can be felt at having not only made a sheet of paper but having picked and processed the fibres as well.

Fibres

It is the cellulose in plant fibres that is needed for papermaking. Many plants are suitable, each giving its own special characteristics. Some produce very little usable fibre for papermaking, whereas others, such as the New Zealand flax plant, give a high percentage. Large quantities are needed as most of the plant breaks down during processing, and at least a bucketful should be gathered.

In cities, a market is an excellent place for picking up the right plant fibres. Pineapple leaves, corn husks, gladioli, iris and daffodil leaves are all suitable. In the countryside there is a greater choice: pampas grass, nettle stems, rush, straw, and montbretia, to name but a few. To recognize suitable plants for papermaking, observe the leaf structure: long, tough vertical strands of fibre are ideal.

Preparation

For how to prepare the plant fibres follow the step-by-step instructions overleaf.

Beating

After preparing the plant fibres, place a handful of rinsed fibres on the board and add some water. Beat with the mallet or flat side of the stone. The fibres will separate and feather out slightly. If making sheets from fibres only, beat until well disintegrated. Put beaten fibres in the tub and proceed to make paper as previously described. Adding a capful of fabric conditioner to the tub of fibres aids couching, which can be difficult with long, tangly strands of fibre. A blender can be used to break down fibres instead of the mallet or stone. However the blender cuts the fibres rather than feathering them out

in the way preferred for papermaking.

Bleaching

The natural colour of fibres is not always desirable. Bleaching can lighten them, and this is best done when the rinsing is partially finished.

Safety

Always wear gloves and an apron when using chemicals such as bleach and caustic soda. Work in the garden or in a well ventilated room and immediately wash off any drops that fall on your skin. Always add caustic soda carefully to water – never pour water on it.

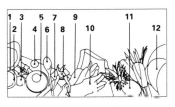

Equipment checklist

1 caustic soda or soda ash (sodium carbonate) crystals
2 bleach
3 wooden board (or formica)
4 pH strip, available from chemist shops
5 scales
6 wooden spoon
7 wooden mallet (or flat stone)
8 pruning shears (or scissors)
9 apron
10 rubber gloves
11 plant fibres
12 stainless steel bucket with lid

Also needed: kitchen blender, electric hot plate or gas ring, sieve and netting.

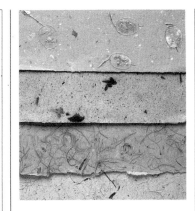

Examples of papers made using pulp containing fibres.

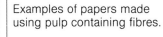

Preparation

Don't rush the fibre preparation process – chemicals are dangerous and need to be handled with great care. Above all, you will need to work in a well ventilated room to disperse the fumes. Better still is to carry out the process outdoors, simmering the fibres on a portable electric hotplate or Calor Gas stove.

1 Cut fibres to 2.5cm (1in) strips and weigh.

2 Place in stainless steel bucket and cover with cold water.

3 Add 2 per cent caustic soda to the dry weight of the fibres or 15 per cent if using soda crystals. Mix with the spoon.

4 Bring to the boil and simmer, with the lid on, for two hours.

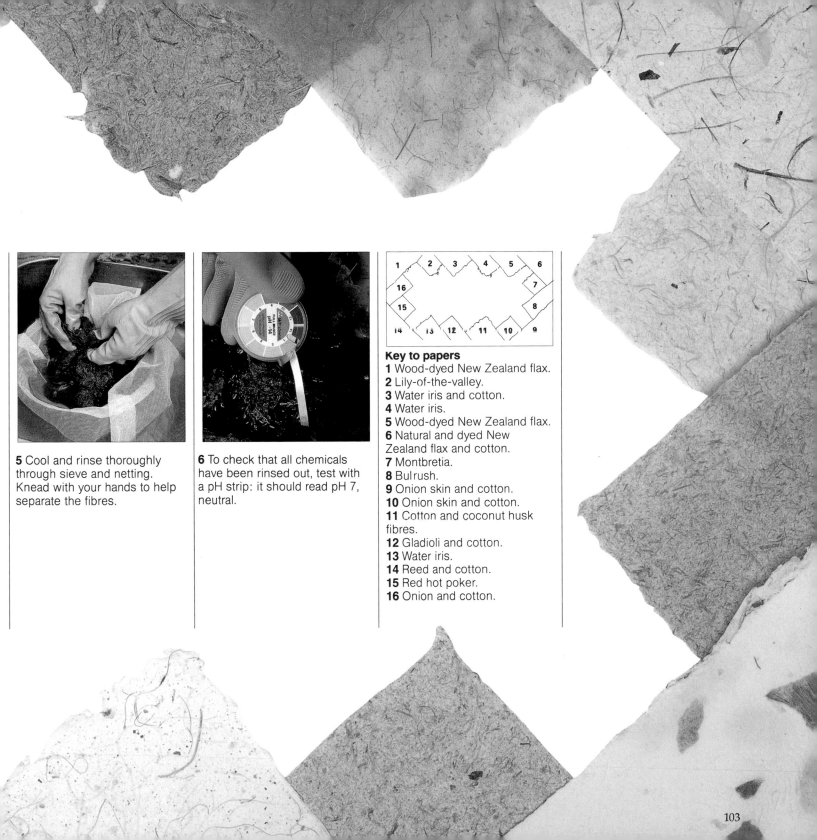

5 Cool and rinse thoroughly through sieve and netting. Knead with your hands to help separate the fibres.

6 To check that all chemicals have been rinsed out, test with a pH strip: it should read pH 7, neutral.

Key to papers
1 Wood-dyed New Zealand flax.
2 Lily-of-the-valley.
3 Water iris and cotton.
4 Water iris.
5 Wood-dyed New Zealand flax.
6 Natural and dyed New Zealand flax and cotton.
7 Montbretia.
8 Bulrush.
9 Onion skin and cotton.
10 Onion skin and cotton.
11 Cotton and coconut husk fibres.
12 Gladioli and cotton.
13 Water iris.
14 Reed and cotton.
15 Red hot poker.
16 Onion and cotton.

Creative papermaking is a comparatively new art form and is still developing, reaching into many other areas of art. With the revival of papermaking in recent decades, some papermakers have specialized in high-quality papers for artists, printers and bookbinders. Others make papers that are beautiful objects in themselves, richly textured and sometimes shaped.

Colouring pulp
Pulp can be coloured with textile dyes. Cold-water dyes need a week for the colour to be fully absorbed. Remember to rinse thoroughly. A simpler way to achieve coloured pulp is to recycle coloured papers.

Porridge technique
This is great fun and is best done with several colours.

Strain off coloured, porridge-textured pulp. Using your hands, place the pulp directly onto a rigid clean surface, such as Formica or perspex. Place coloured pulps down next to one another. Colours can be put down in any order and not necessarily in a rectangular format. When the image is ready, place a sheet of interfacing on top and gently press out excess water with a sponge. This helps bonding and speeds drying. Leave to air dry.

Two-coloured sheet
Make up two tubs of pulp, one of each colour. Couch a sheet from one colour. Partially dip the mould into the other tub and couch this on top of the base sheet.

Encapsulation
Pulp can act as a glue. By laying flat objects onto a base sheet and then partially or totally covering them with pulp from the turkey baster, they are held in place.

Pressed flowers and leaves
Pressed flowers and leaves can look very attractive in a sheet. First seal with artist's fixative, so that they do not "bleed" colour onto the sheet.

Pastry cutters
Pulp can be poured through a pastry cutter to make a definite shape. This is best done on the mould or interfacing before couching or transferring onto the base sheet.

Sandwich method
Couch a base sheet. Lay threads, feathers or any relatively flat objects on top. Couch a second sheet on top of this, thereby making a sandwich of the objects. This can be left as it is, or some of the pulp from the top sheet can be gently taken off to expose the middle layer.

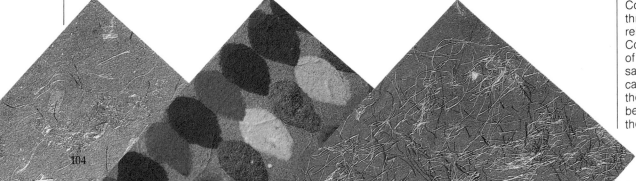

Pouring pulp

Differently coloured pulps can be separated into plastic containers and used like an artist's palette. In place of a brush, a turkey baster makes it easier to suck up pulp and deposit it on a base sheet (a freshly made sheet of paper). The pouring can be done directly onto the base sheet or couched off the mould. Poured pulp can be built up in several layers, which will magically stick together during the pressing.

Embossing

Because pulp is a malleable substance, it easily picks up textures when pressed. Lay a textured piece of lace onto a freshly made sheet, cover with interfacing and felt for padding. Press. Leave the sheet to dry with or without the lace on.

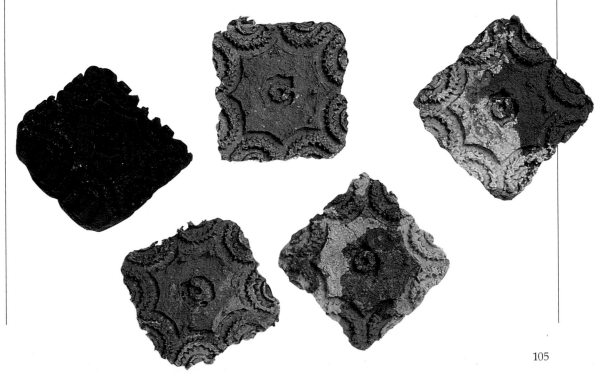

DECOUPAGE

Decoupage is a French word meaning "cut out". The art was developed as a pastime by ladies of the eighteenth-century French Court who used cut-out printed paper motifs to decorate wooden boxes, in imitation of the oriental lacquered boxes that were popular at the time.

The technique is very simple. The traditional method is carefully to cut out a flower, figure, animal or other motif from a coloured print, then to glue it, singly or with others, to a wooden surface, such as a box. The paper is protected by many layers of clear varnish to create an inlaid effect similar to that of marquetry. The paper appears to be "in" the wood, not on the surface.

In modern times the technique has broadened to take account of contemporary tastes and new materials. Now, decoupage includes any means of forming a paper surface, such as creating a paper mosaic, using typography or making abstract compositions. Magazine photographs, old catalogues, posters and calendars are excellent and inexpensive sources for motifs.

For a smooth surface, it is important to ensure that all the papers are of equal thickness. Stick the papers down with PVA glue, applied liberally. Traditionally, the cut outs were sunk beneath 15 to 20 coats of varnish, but modern clear polyurethane varnishes give the same effect with 10 to 15 layers. Use a varnish with a gloss finish. Allow each coat to dry, and wipe the surface clean before applying the next. Lightly sand down each coat after the tenth, using fine sandpaper. If a less sunken effect is wanted, use fewer coats.

Decoupage is an inexpensive and creative way to brighten up surfaces such as an old box, cupboard, tray, screen or mirror frame. The coverage can be minimal – perhaps as a pattern around the edge of a surface – or total, as a dense collage. The surface may be painted or stained before the cut-outs are applied.

SUE MATTHEWS
Decoupage table
This simple but striking geometric design was achieved by making several large mosaics of paper pieces torn from magazine photographs, each mosaic of a different colour.
Table area: 50×40cm (20×16in)

MODEL MAKING

Model-making with paper and card is the equivalent of modelling in plastic, wood, metal or any other material. Whatever the medium, the common aim is to reproduce a building or other man-made object as an accurate scale model.

Until recently, paper and card were used extensively by architects and engineers to make scale models of projects for building approval. Such models were frequently painted to show stonework, rivets and the like. Today, professional model-makers prefer to use plastics and soft wood. However, the advantages of paper and card to the amateur model-maker are clear: they are inexpensive, easy to work and decorate and require little equipment or space.

Planning and materials
The secret of model-making is to have a good set of plans, photographs or drawings, so that accurate measurements can be taken. It is also important to know which weight of paper or card would be appropriate for which part of the model. For example, if a scale model of a building is being made, a lintel across the top of a window can be shown by gluing a thick piece of card to the wall, creating the illusion of protruding stone. Extra thicknesses can be represented by laminating sheets of card together, then sanding the edges with fine sandpaper. Polyboard (a sandwich of foam and card) may be used as an alternative to laminating; it is strong but cuts easily.

Always use a very sharp scalpel when cutting the paper or card, renewing the blade regularly. Use a strong, quick-drying glue or cement. Draw the measurements with a hard pencil on the reverse side of the card to keep the outer surface clean. If the card is to be painted, most model-makers cut out all the pieces, check them for accuracy, then paint them *before* they are cemented together. This is easier than painting onto the assembled model, though finishing touches may be added at the end.

DAMIEN JOHNSTON
Chapel
The model was built from a drawing in an architectural source book. The play of light and shade over the card creates sufficient interest for colour to be unnecessary.
Height: 37cm (15in)

PAPER ENGINEERING

Paper engineering (or cardboard engineering, as it is sometimes called) is a catch-all name given to several commercial paper arts, including MODEL MAKING, PACKAGE DESIGN, POP-UPS and pre-made cardboard store-window or in-store advertising displays. The term "engineering" is used because these paperworks are designed with careful regard to a cost-effective manufacturing process and the technical limitations imposed either by machines that stamp the creases then glue and fold the card, or hand-assembly. It is a measure of the skills of paper engineers that, despite these severe limitations to their creativity, work of remarkable ingenuity is not uncommon. Professional paper engineers usually create their designs to a brief given by a client or employer. Some are patented.

Making "explosives"
The techniques of model making, package design and pop-ups are described elsewhere in this book. Another – and extraordinary – paper engineering technique is that of elastic-powered pop-ups, sometimes called "explosives".

The basic principle is to construct a three-dimensional solid, then to squash it flat. When 3-D, an elastic band is attached to two distant points that will move apart when the solid is flattened, pulling the band very taut. The 2-D shape is held flat inside an envelope, but when it is taken out, the elastic contracts, snapping the 3-D form vigorously and unexpectedly back into shape.

The drama and humour of these constructions makes them ideal for postal promotions. Strong card must be used, because the forces involved are surprisingly powerful and thin card would buckle. With planning, integral card hooks can be constructed inside the solid to hold the elastic band in place.

There are a surprising number of ways to collapse simple 3-D forms, though not all are suitable for commercial manufacture. Experiment with a cube or pyramid by slitting along edges or across a diagonal on a face to see how many ways the form can be flattened. Then decide which points should be connected by an elastic band, and re-make the design using strong card.

Exploding hexagonal box
1 The box is here shown split open down the sides and squashed flat. An elastic band is stretched taut between a pair of opposite edges, so that the shape remains flat only with pressure.

2 With a release of downward pressure, the elastic begins to contract with surprising force. This happens almost instantly when the flat shape is removed from an envelope. In time though, the elastic will perish if the shape is held flat for too long, so that eventually, the pop-up mechanism will weaken.

Exploding pyramid

1 The square pyramid is here shown flat, the base having been split open along a diagonal to enable the 3-D form to flatten. An elastic band connects opposite corners and is stretched taut when the pyramid is flattened. Pressure from the hand keeps it flat.

2 Semi-erected. The square base can be seen opening across the bottom right of the structure. If the restraining hand is released quickly, the force within the elastic is such that the pyramid erects itself while doing a double somersault!

3 The box is here shown in its "resting" position. Because the top and bottom faces remain flat, box may be placed on box to achieve a double or treble spring action of remarkable height. (Design copyright Karran Products Ltd.)

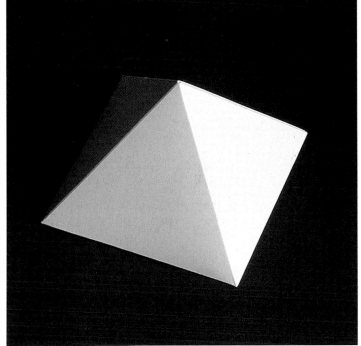

3 Erect. The pyramid is now in its stable position: all forces are at rest. Pyramids with different numbers of faces may also be constructed, though the geometry of the mechanism may be difficult to control. (Design copyright Karran Products Ltd.)

PAPER CUTS

Decorative paper cuts dating from AD 207 have been found in northern China, and it is thought that the Chinese were cutting paper long before that. Paper cutting is a tradition in many other countries too, notably, Japan, Mexico, Poland, Germany, Switzerland, The Netherlands and in areas of Dutch influence in the United States, such as Pennsylvania.

Unlike DECOUPAGE, which began with the use of existing paper motifs, paper cutters use traditional designs or evolve their own. The term covers the creation of figurative or abstract shapes and the folding and cutting of paper to make repeat patterns of an almost magical quality for decorative purposes as well as for making mobiles and collages.

Originally paper cuts were connected with religious and ceremonial observances, but when paper became more plentiful, paper pictures were pasted on walls, furniture and windows to brighten up the home. The cutters depicted familiar flowers and animals, and illustrated stories and legends. In the late nineteenth century the cutting of paper portraits became popular in Western countries, and itinerant artists cut sometimes very humorous silhouettes of individuals and family groups. Silhouette cutting was a popular home hobby, too, but declined with the development of photography.

Cutting with scissors

Paper may be cut with scissors or a knife, each tool providing slightly different effects. Scissors may vary in size from the bulky sheep shears used in Poland to the delicate manicure-type scissors preferred by silhouettists. The technique for cutting with scissors is to hold the paper in the air, grasp the scissors firmly with one hand and move the paper into the blades with the other hand. In this way, smooth curves result. Sharply angled corners are cut with the tip of the scissors. The paper may be a single sheet or be folded once or several times to produce symmetrical cut-outs.

Cutting with a knife

A scalpel or craft knife should be used, and these are readily available from art and craft shops. Above all, the blade must be sharp. The paper should rest on a resilient

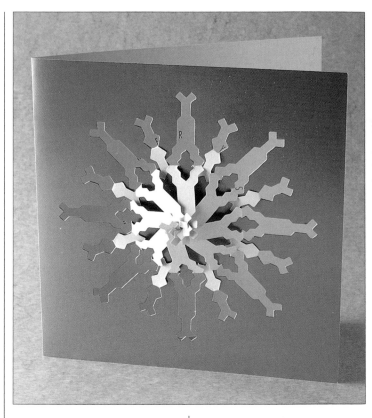

LYN HOURAHINE/PAPER POWER
Snowflake card
This is not a traditional example of an image cut from paper, but one in which ingenious use is made of cut-out shapes. Eight large Y shapes are cut out and folded back to interlock in the centre, trapping eight small I units beneath. The result is a beautiful negative/positive image that makes full use of the two-colour (coated) card.
Height: 18cm (7in)

surface for cutting, and several layers may be stacked to produce multiples.

Papers may also be torn to provide additional interest with their ragged edges.

Symmetrical designs

Long-established techniques, including simple methods practised by children and magicians, can be used in controlled or unexpected ways. Cutting snowflakes is always great fun, yet the ingenious technique of cutting paper which has been folded in quarters or eighths can be used to produce dramatic, rhythmic patterns. Magicians have long known how to grow an instant tree from newspaper with only three cuts. This and other paper tricks can be adapted for making large wall decorations and sculptural mobiles that express the cutter's own inspiration.

Collages

Some paper cutters relate more closely to prevailing trends in art by designing with found papers or decorating white paper which is cut and pasted onto a strong paper background. Others may like to follow the example of Henri Matisse, who covered large sheets of paper with gouache in the exact shades he desired and shaped and combined them into works that he considered the purest expression of colour.

Contemporary artists who cut shapes into collages, however, often rely on the large choice of colourful patterns from magazines, giftwraps, handmade papers and many other resources.

The professional paper cutters of today are the graphic artists who cut designs to be reproduced anonymously in newspapers, magazines, travel brochures and on greetings cards, posters and carrier bags. Keeping an eye on their work is a useful way to glean fresh ideas of your own.

TRADITIONAL CHINESE
Grasses
▲ The paper is cut in an extraordinarily delicate way to create an image of great beauty. In particular, the length of the stems requires great skill to cut so that the sections align. The paper is extremely thin, yet strong.
Height: 10cm (4in)

JACK YATES
Group portrait
Jack Yates combines the western tradition of stained glass with paper cuts. The basic paper cut resembles a stencil, on the underside of which is pasted coloured paper.

QUILLING

Quilling is the art of rolling paper strips and applying them to a background to create abstract or figurative designs. It may have originated in Ancient Egypt, but the first clear reference to the art is in fifteenth-century England, where it was used by poor ecclesiastical organizations to provide backgrounds to religious sculptures, in imitation of the gold and silver filigree (ornamental work of fine wire) used by wealthier institutions. The art was revived in the seventeenth century by ladies of leisure, who used it to decorate workboxes, screens, cabinets and the like. It has fallen from favour and been revived several times since, and like many papercrafts, it is currently enjoying a revival.

The origin of the name "quilling" is unclear. It could come from the quill pen, into whose split end a paper strip was inserted prior to being rolled, or from the porcupine quill, used as a needle by North American Indians when decorating moccasins with animal hair in a filigree manner.

BRENDA RHODES
Box
The quilled decoration uses an old technique known as "huskin". Pins are tapped into the wooden box at specific points, then the paper strips are coiled around them to form the quilled shapes. This differs from the conventional method, because the quilling is done *in situ*.
Diameter: 15cm (6in)

Quilling methods

The technique for quilling is to roll long, narrow strips of paper into one of twenty or so basic shapes, such as the coil, star, tulip, S or feeler, some of which are squashed and creased. The rolling is done either between finger and thumb, or by using a special tool with a split end, into which the end of the paper strip is trapped prior to being rolled (quilled). Papers of different widths may be used to create a relief effect. Different basic shapes require strips of varying lengths.

A strong paper glue is applied to one edge of the quilled strip for sticking to the background. Sometimes no background is used: the quilled shapes are glued to each other, perhaps in imitation of wrought-iron garden furniture.

Densely coiled shapes can be applied to everyday items such as boxes. They form a surprisingly strong surface that will not crush when handled. More open compositions should be protected under glass, but very narrow 2mm ($^1/_{10}$in) strips can be safely glued to greetings cards and mailed.

BRENDA RHODES
Cribbage board
The quilled shapes here form a mosaic of coils which create a delicate dragonfly motif as the centrepiece to a Regency-style cribbage board (modern boards are rectangular, not circular). Note the use of colour, which is not only decorative, but helps define the motif.
Diameter: 15cm (6in)

PACKAGING

As far as paper is concerned, packaging means the making of cartons, and it is a massive industry. Approximately half of all paper pulp is made into card or board for packaging, the other half being used mainly for printing papers. The number of carton designs is almost as varied as the number of products they contain, although there are only a few dozen basic *nets* (the two-dimensional shape from which a carton is folded up and glued). Today, these nets can be stretched or compressed by computer to create cost-effective cartons of any proportion. Cartons of a genuinely original design are rare. And that is one good reason for a craftperson to try designing cartons that are creative and uncommercial, say to package a gift in an entertaining, ingenious or extravagant way.

Making a net
The key to designing a carton is knowing how to form a strong net and where to position the glue tabs so that the carton will lock.

The easiest way to design a net is first to sketch out a carton, then to construct it from separate pieces of card, one per face. Tape the pieces together, edge to edge, then slit open some of the edges until the carton can unfold flat. Whenever possible, slit short edges before long ones: the net will be compact and stronger.

Start tabbing the net with a tab on the middle edge of the lid, then tab *each alternate edge* around the perimeter of the net, measuring deep, square tab shapes. This simple procedure will automatically place all the tabs in the best place to create the strongest possible carton. Essentially, the tabbing system is a formula. For once, do not try to be creative!

Once the net and tabs have been assembled, re-make the carton very accurately from one sheet of card.

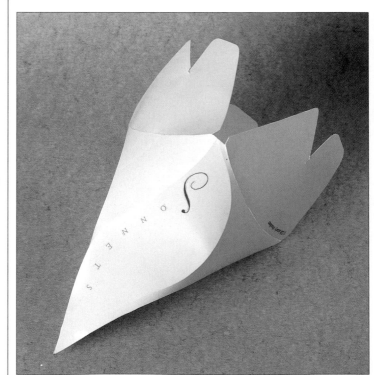

SUZANNE BENNETT
Confectionery box
This box makes use of curved edges, an aspect of packaging that is often overlooked. In fact, many straight edges on commercial packaging can be substituted with curves. (Student project: Ravensbourne College of Design and Communication) Length: 18cm (7in)

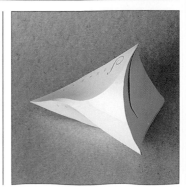

Beautiful boxes

Another way to glean ideas for construction is to take apart commercially manufactured cartons, especially the more inventive Easter and Christmas designs. It is important to think of a carton as something other than a rectangular box, even if technical reasons make this the commonest commercial shape. A hand-made carton may be any shape and take inspiration from many sources. Consider making cartons that are multi-piece, that use curves, or are asymmetric, or which are influenced by crystals, architectural forms or a subject matter of personal interest.

Two-piece box
JANINA DIETZEL
◄ In this packaging study the same locking mechanism is used as in the example above, but the form has been stretched. Curiously, the shape of the join is a perfect hexagon, though this is difficult to perceive once the tabs are added. (Student project: Ravensbourne College of Design and Communication) Length: 13cm (5in)

▲ Here a package is shown assembled and disassembled – both units are identical. The interlocked form shows a clean join. This is achieved by placing a triangular tab onto each alternate edge of the join, which lock beneath the untabbed edge of the opposing unit. Thus, each unit has three tabbed and three untabbed edges which elegantly interlace to create a satisfying lock.

ABSTRACT

GEOMETRIC FORMS • NON-GEOMETRIC FORMS

S o-called abstract images in any medium are broadly of two kinds: those that derive from, or allude to, a subject in the real world or an emotion; and those that have no direct origin in reality, but are pieces of work to be enjoyed simply for what they are. In artistic jargon the two kinds are labelled "abstract" and "non-figurative": "abstract" because an image is abstracted from an identifiable source, and "non-figurative" where an image does not derive from the figurative (or recognized) world. In this chapter, Roll it and Heaven's gate are abstractions, whereas the pieces opposite are both non-figurative. The distinction may seem pedantic, but the terms identify wholly separate creative practices.

The chapter is divided into two sections: GEOMETRIC FORMS and NON-GEOMETRIC FORMS. Both contain examples of abstract and non-figurative work, but the characters of the two sections are very different. Geometric work is typified by straight lines, repeats, verticals, horizontals, symmetry, ingenuity and the linking of creativity with geometric or engineering principles. The pieces are usually logical and constructed according to a system or set of rules. They are frequently made from bought papers. This apparent rigour can create work of a timeless beauty that transcends cultures and fashions in pieces that betray little direct evidence of the artist's ego. It may sometimes seem that the pieces were always there in the paper, waiting to be released.

By contrast, the NON-GEOMETRIC FORMS section of the chapter contains work of a far more personal nature. Here the pieces are organic, spontaneous, textured, emotive and individual-istic, conveying more of the artist's own particular vision, calling more directly to the senses and summoning a more immedi-ately emotional response.

The work that follows demonstrates both the variety of papercraft techniques and the range of creative expression the material can offer when it is applied to abstract and non-figurative images and objects.

GEOMETRIC FORMS

The flatness of paper makes it the ideal material with which to design geometric forms: better than volumetric materials, such as wood, clay or metals, which need considerable craft skills to achieve the precision that geometry demands. Paper can achieve this precision with ease.

The work that follows divides into two broad categories: pieces that are constructed according to geometric principles, and those that are geometric in appearance but which are constructed intuitively. Both the pieces on this page are examples of the former category: their forms, though perhaps found by what might be termed "informed doodling", nevertheless obey the principles of geometry to hold their shape. In the intuitive category are Untitled, Echoes IV and Rectangular Composition, which are constructed according to their creators' own judgements.

Note also the use of colour, sometimes wholly absent and sometimes employed in a vivid manner, contradicting the common assumption that geometric work should be cool and dispassionate.

GUY HOUDOUIN
Patak au paradis

◀ The extraordinarily intricate centre to the piece is made by overlapping many differently coloured sheets of paper, incising through the layers in a strictly defined pattern, then folding back the layers and trapping them flat beneath "belts" of paper on the top layer. The effect is a scintillating explosion of colour that is a little different on each arm of the star. See also Patak I révolutionnaire by the same artist.
Diameter: approximately 150cm (58in)

DAVID MITCHELL/DAVE BRILL
Enigma cube

▶ A jointly created piece, this example of modular ORIGAMI is unusual because its structure incorporates curves. Twelve identically folded squares are interlocked without glue to form a cube, seemingly embedded within a larger, curved form. The bold shapes and intriguing interplay between the straight and curved edges create a memorable work of creative geometry. As a bonus, the modules are simple to make and lock strongly.
Height: 11cm (4½in)

JO BLOK
Pentagonal structure

▲ What appears to be a complex solid is made from 12 simple, identical modules that interlock without glue. Each module is based on a pentangle (a five-sided star) with a curved hook to one side of each corner to lock with other corners. The complete structure totally encloses a negative solid at its centre, which is a dodecahedron. (Student project: Richmond upon Thames College.)
Diameter: 15cm (6in)

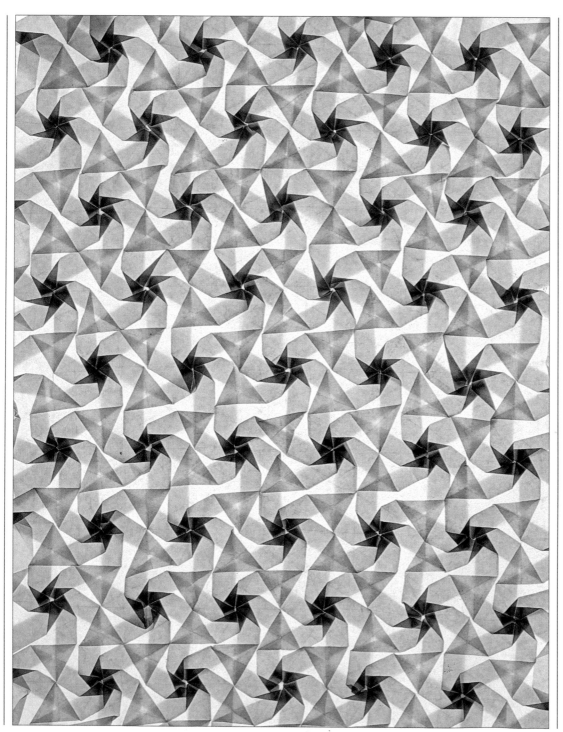

SHUZO FUJIMOTO
120° twist origami
This beautiful example of pre-creased ORIGAMI using the technology technique is made from a single sheet of translucent tissue paper and is back lit. Its companion piece (opposite) is made in a similar way. The six-pointed stars and the regular triangles indicate that the tissue was pre-creased into the unusual grid of 120° and 60° creases. The creases must be located with a great accuracy and collapsed one by one across the sheet. The stars are folded later. The artist has designed a great number of twist patterns, some of which may be placed side-by-side on the same sheet.
30×20cm (12×8in)

SHUZO FUJIMOTO
90° twist origami
The companion of the 120°
piece shown opposite. This
piece is collapsed flat from the
conventional 90° and 45° grid of
creases used throughout the
technology ORIGAMI technique.
The artist uses the word "twist"
to describe his work because
each repeat of a pattern is
formed at the intersection of a
number of pleats that travel
across the paper. The paper is
collapsed flat by being twisted,
so that the pleats radiate away
symmetrically from the
intersection.
30×20cm (12×8in)

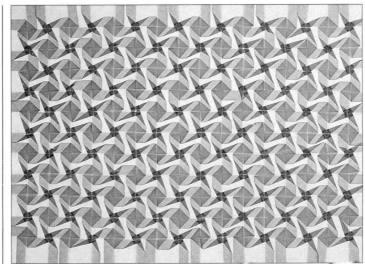

JOAN STERRENBURG
Big checker
One of a series of similar
pieces, each layer is made from
handmade coloured abaca fibre
paper, secured at the back for
transportation and exhibition.
The geometric grid is
countered by the texture of the
paper and the rich use of
colour.
197×91cm (79×45in)

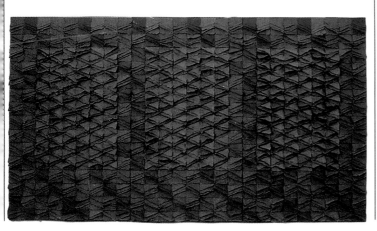

TOSHIKAZU KAWASAKI
Rose crystallization
▶ These pieces are closely
related to Fujimoto's twist
designs on these two pages.
They are made from uncut
squares of paper, first folded
into a particular grid of pre-
creases, then collapsed into
shape. The difference is that,
instead of being flat, they are
three-dimensional. A sheet with
more repetitions of the crease
pattern would permit a block
with a larger number of roses to
be folded. The strictures of the
system are pleasingly tempered
by the curved shape of the
internal walls, which are a little
wobbly.
4.5×4.5×1cm (1³⁄₄×1³⁄₄×¹⁄₂in)

HIDEAKI TOMOOKA
Shri-yantra
▶ This piece in the series is made solely by pricking the sheet. Needles of different widths create holes with different diameters. The technique is not unlike drawing, with the density and size of the holes resembling the outline or the light and shade of an image.
50×50cm (19½×19½in)

HIDEAKI TOMOOKA
Shri-yantra
▼ One of a series of eight (another is right), these serene pieces achieve their entire impact from the way in which light falls across their surface. A strong frontal light would render them almost invisible, whereas an even side light – such as that from a window – would cast shadows. The effect is obtained by pricking the surface and by indenting from the back with a blunt implement to create a ridge.
50×50cm (19½×19½in)

KISABURO KAWAKAMI
Echoes IV
Another piece by the same artist appears on the preceding pages. The similarity between the two is apparent, though they are clearly made by very different techniques. The relief image is achieved by embossing the paper. A copper plate is etched with the design, then pressed into the paper from the back, so that the unetched surface of the plate forms the raised surface on the front of the sheet. Less precise embossings can be made by placing cardboard shapes under the paper and burnishing the front with the bowl of a spoon. The paper will stretch better over the cardboard or etched plate if it is dampened first and is unsized.
35×35cm (14×14in)

JEAN-CLAUDE CORREIA
Le Manteau de Montezuma
▼ Here Correia has folded an immense sheet (450×100cm/180×39in) into a 3-D form of great textural beauty. The large scale and dense repetitions typical of much of the artist's work create a weight and energy unique in paper folding. 110×80×20cm (45×32×8in)

JEAN-CLAUDE CORREIA
Trois rides
▲ The artist is a professional paper folder – one of very few who make a living from their creations. He insists that his work is not *origami* – which he sees as essentially a model-making technique derived from Japanese tradition – but his creations are folded from uncut sheets. His technique is similar to that of Fujimoto and Kawasaki, but the result is more than decorative. Before folding, the paper is covered with acrylic and crayon to hide the manufactured surface and to increase the status of the work as art.
75×55×3cm (30×22×1in)

PAUL JACKSON
Bulge
Fundamentally a very simple piece, this folded structure is made by covering a square in a carefully laid out grid of pre-creases, then alternately pleating two adjacent edges, so that the pleats continually criss-cross along the diagonal. The bulge occurs naturally and the creases lock under their own tension. To the artist, the piece is more "discovered" than created, such is the seeming simplicity of its construction and the purity of its form. The same principle can be applied to many other pleated configurations. See also the Crumple forms by the same artist.
22×22×10cm (9×9×4in)

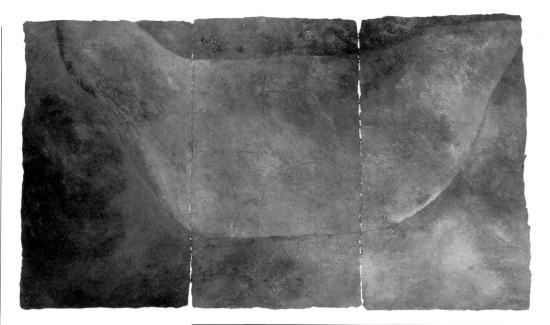

NANCY THAYER
Peace for Paul
▼ Here, cotton PAPER PULP is poured onto a foamboard base, which remains part of the finished piece, both for extra strength and to help hang the work. Acrylic paint is applied to the surface when dry. Another work by the same artist is on the facing page.
142×107cm (58×44in)

CAROL FARROW
Underground vessel
▲ Made in a similar manner to the work on the facing page by the same artist, this large triptych of HANDMADE PAPER, painted with acrylic and waxed, is perhaps the most unstructured but sensual image in the book. See also Five implements by the same artist.
233×135cm (95×55in)

NANCY THAYER
Heaven's gate

◄ This piece is made in a similar way to Peace for Paul on the facing page. The image has Mayan and Egyptian influences, which the artist has used to symbolize a language common to all peoples of all cultures, arising out of the shared concerns of life, death, health, God and nature.
170×85cm (69×34in)

CAROL FARROW
Just beneath the surface

▼ The large scale of this piece is achieved through collage, by making sheets of paper, painting them, and then embedding them in a wet, white cotton linter pulp base. The assemblage Is allowed to dry, is sized, then painted again with water based paints. Thus, much of the surface is paint, not paper.
257×257cm (101×101in)

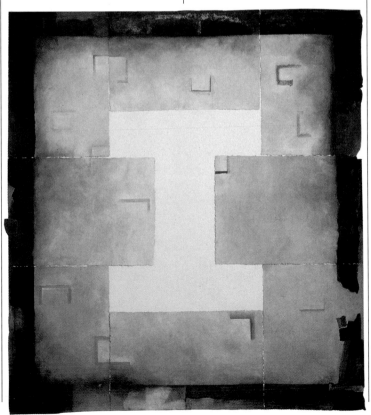

PAUL JACKSON
Crumple form
◀ This piece (and the one on the right) shows how creases can be used not only to form a structure, but also to create a surface texture. The technique is to use very thin paper that can hold a crease, such as airmail paper, layout pad paper or – ideally – Bible paper: the thinner the paper, the better it crumples. In this example, the sheet was glued to form a cylinder, then repeatedly crumpled and re-opened until it was full of crumples and greatly reduced in size. The rib creases were then carefully pulled out from the crumpled surface to create an organic, semi-improvised form, quite unlike anything possible with conventional ORIGAMI techniques.
Height: 20cm (8in)

PAUL JACKSON
Crumple form
▶ Similar to the work on the facing page, this form uses a different crumpling technique. Here, the uncreased paper is held at a corner and allowed to hang, then gathered together rather like the furls of an umbrella, so that the crumples radiate from the held corner. More radiating crumples are put in, then mountain and valley rib creases are stretched through them to create any number of concentric horizontal lips. Other crumpling techniques can be used to produce entirely different effects.
Height: 28cm (11in)

VANESSA GODFREY
Thistle cycle
▼ This bold work is an example of the PAPER PULP technique. Recycled pulp was poured onto a flat surface and the thistle and elder leaves were embedded into it while it was still wet. The growth cycle of the plants is symbolized by the lengthening of the stalks around the centre. The recycling of the pulp – which is itself plant fibre – extends the theme to create a rich yet simple piece. Another work by the same artist is on the facing page.
47×38cm (18½×15in)

GUY HOUDOUIN
Patak I révolutionnaire
▲ This complex piece, simultaneously controlled yet energetic, is made by WEAVING together many coloured strips of twisted paper, painted on both sides. The colours are mostly primary or near-primary, but mix optically when woven to create the illusion of secondary and tertiary colours. The artist has produced a number of similar pieces, some made from single sheets of paper that are shredded almost to the centre and woven, rather than woven from separate strips. See also Patak au paradis by the same artist.
Diameter: 120cm (49in)

MARY BIRD
Swedish rug

◀ The rug/wallhanging was knitted as a series of 21cm (9in) squares using very large needles and three 2cm (¾in) wide strips of paper. Then the knitted squares were laced together at the back to assemble the rug (though the joins are all but invisible). Black and white crêpe paper was used for strength, and beige kitchen paper for texture and colour. The fringe was made by knotting strips to the edge of the rug. (Student project: School of Art and Design, Swindon College.)
154×66cm (63×27in)

VANESSA GODFREY
Pyramid

Coloured PAPER PULP was poured onto a flat surface in layers to create the main image, into which pink hydrangea flowers were embedded in a regular grid, while the pulp was wet. The contrast between the poured blue pulp lines and the "found" pink flowers created a dynamic yet subtle image. Another piece by the same artist is on the facing page.
41×34cm (16½×13½in)

GJERTRUD HALS
Lava

Are these extraordinary bowl forms functional? Yes, but not in the conventional sense. When not being exhibited collectively as an installation piece, they are used by dancers, who throw them and lie on them as part of their performance. The remarkable strength of these sculptures is achieved by the PAPER PULP technique. First, a cardboard mould is made and coated with plastic. Then the pulp – a mixture of cotton, flax, sisal, local grasses and silk, strengthened with cheesecloth – is applied. The fibres are dyed to give colour. Some bowls are waxed.
Height: approximately 110cm (43in)

GILLIAN JOHNSON-FLINT
Lynette with her dog
▶ The image is a watermark formed in handmade paper. It is achieved by carefully sewing the design into a piece of loose nylon with a needle and fine fishing line. The nylon piece is then trapped between the frames of a papermaker's conventional mould and deckle (see PAPERMAKING), so that when a piece of paper is formed, the pulp lies more thinly over the sewn fishing line. This creates a translucent line, which can be read as the watermark.
Paper size: 21×26cm (8×10in)

MADELEINE CHILD
Breakfast-in-bed tray (with jam jars)
▲ This witty, semi-functional piece is made by the PAPER PULP technique. The mould is made from layers of polyboard and wire, covered in pulp, then decorated with acrylic to give a permanent finish. The handles and feet are securely attached, and the layered polyboard makes the tray strong enough to support the weight of breakfast crockery.
90×35×20cm (36×14×8in)

KEVIN PERRY/PAPER POWER
for SECOND NATURE
Bunch of flowers
This commercially manufactured greeting card is one of a series using the "explosive" principle described in PAPER ENGINEERING. The basic form is a four-sided tube, flattened inside a wallet. As the form is removed from the wallet, an elastic mechanism inside the tube contracts, instantly creating the 3-D form of the card. The flowers are formed by a combination of pleated paper and INCISED POP-UP cut-away techniques. The wings to each side fold up and protect the flowers when the card is two-dimensional.
Height: 18cm (7in)

JANET WILSON
Chess pieces
An unusual example of QUILLING, these pieces are made using pleasingly simple techniques. The bodies are solid coils of paper, one inside another, and the tops are basic quilled forms.
Life size

KEVIN PERRY/PAPER POWER
Christmas tree
Produced as a Christmas card to send to clients, this design makes ingenious use of the collapsing trellis principle. The reflective card doubles the number of facets seen by the viewer and creates the illusion of the design extending beyond the back layer of card.
23×23×10cm (9×9×4in)

KEVIN PERRY/KEE SCOTT
"Explosive" house
A fine example of "explosive" PAPER ENGINEERING, this elastic-powered multi-piece pop-up was designed as a mail shot to make potential customers aware of a new mortgage package. The basic shape of the house is a square-on box, capped by a roof. When the structure is collapsed flat, a thick elastic band (which can just be glimpsed in the middle photograph) is stretched taut along the central axis. The elastic contracts when the house is removed from the restraining envelope in which it was mailed, so instantly erecting the pop-up.
19×15×12cm (7½×6×5in)

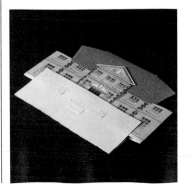
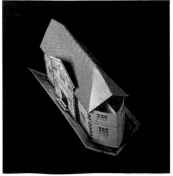

PAUL ELPHICK
180° pop-up
Design of this MULTI-PIECE POP-UP developed from a poster publicizing an exhibition of student work. Much use is made of the multi-piece layering technique to create a series of levels onto which the bold graphic and typographic elements are layered. Note the interesting use of complex silhouettes, the glossy black card to reflect the layers above, and the shaped outline of the base sheet. (Student project: Ravensbourne College of Design and Communication.) 54×22cm (21×9in)

KEIKO NAKAZAWA
Copse
This delicate INCISED POP-UP is made from a single pleated sheet folded like the letter W. The outer strokes remain uncut and are glued to a base card for strength. The inner strokes are allowed to rise vertically to create the subtle relief effect, formed by the generations technique. The piece is equally effective seen from the back. Base card: 20×15cm (8×6in)

MASAHIRO CHATANI
Arches
The artist has written many beautiful POP-UP books and produced a series of commercially available greeting cards, one of which is shown here. The beautiful effect is created entirely from a single sheet of card, using the generations technique. The artist has used the same technique to produce a design depicting an avenue of trees with overhanging branches. 15×10cm (6×4in)

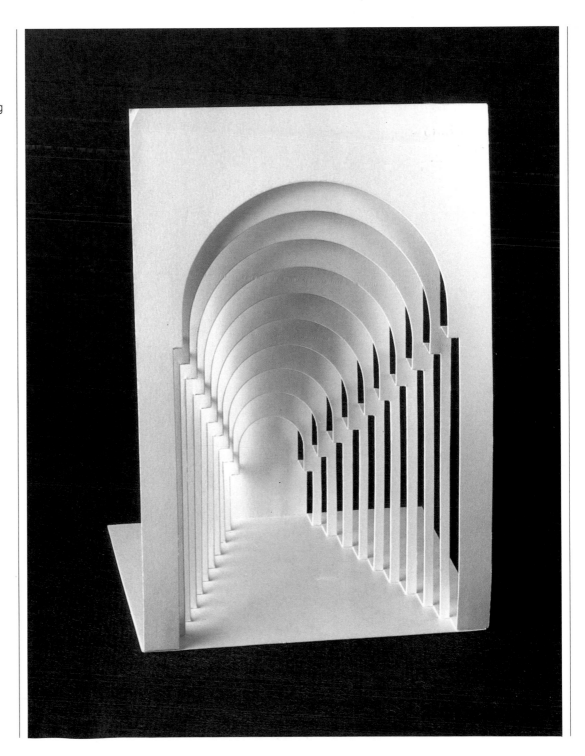

PAUL JOHNSON
Wall cupboard

This large, exuberant and fantastical furniture sculpture is made by cutting and gluing cardboard to create a strong structure onto which pre-decorated sheets of paper are laminated. Inspiration for the piece came from Eastern architecture and ornamentation, and from the fancy of the Gothic revival.
250×71×23cm (99×28×9in)

GILLIAN SPIRES (paper)
ALAN PETERS OBE (carpentry)
Friendship screen

▶ The black Japanese character for "friendship" is not painted or printed onto the handmade paper as might be expected, but is paper itself. Pulp is dyed black then formed on a mould and deckle in the traditional way, except that in this instance, the mould has a stencil laid onto it so that pulp is deposited onto the mould *only* where the stencil does not cover it, thus forming the shape of the character. The pulp is allowed to dry, then embedded into a sheet of white flax pulp. The frame – also beautifully made – is constructed from ebonized teak.
235×161cm (66×96in)

REPRESENTATIONAL

FIGURATIVE • NATURAL WORLD
CONSTRUCTED WORLD • CREATURES

The visual representation or interpretation of the world around us has been the predominant theme for creative artists since earliest times. Yet only recently has paper begun to play a fuller part in this tradition. The history of paper is primarily the story of its role as a functional material, not of its use as a representational medium, although there are exceptions.

In recent decades, the representational possibilities of paper have begun to be explored in a much more intensive way across all techniques, notably in ORIGAMI, PAPER SCULPTURE and PAPIER MÂCHÉ, each for different reasons. Origami has been created by amateurs for the sheer enjoyment of it; paper sculpture has been used by commercial artists and papier mâché by craftspeople and fine artists. Other traditional techniques have been rediscovered while techniques such as making images with paper pulp are among the newest to have become popular.

The four sections of this chapter cover the range of representational categories. The differences between them make for an interesting series of comparisons. For example, the FIGURATIVE section contains works with great expression, whereas the seemingly similar CREATURES section includes pieces that are surprisingly impassive and apparently closer to models or illustrations. This contrast arises from the innate creative response to the themes themselves and from the techniques used to realize them rather than being due to any inherent limitations of paper as a medium.

In the NATURAL WORLD and CONSTRUCTED WORLD sections the work obligingly divides into the two now familiar groups of dry papercraft models and wet papercraft art. It would be an interesting exercise to attempt a cross-over: to make an emotively charged sculpture or image with a dry papercraft – such as an origami design of an angry dog; or to use a naturally expressive wet papercraft to depict some everyday inanimate object.

The human figure is the easiest subject for artists to bring alive, because we see parts of ourselves reflected in it. Not surprisingly, therefore, this is the area in which the paperworks have the most character and emotion, demonstrating how the inertness of paper as a material can be overcome.

The paperworks that follow depict a wide range of techniques and moods. While pieces such as Weekend wear (opposite) and The primitive Methodists display an engaging wit, others such as Horny little devil and Harpy are altogether more disturbing. The range of techniques places a clear emphasis on the more malleable, wet papercrafts of PAPIER MÂCHÉ and PAPER PULP. Of the dry papercrafts, only PAPER SCULPTURE is represented, perhaps because it is the least geometric and so better suited to the theme.

MARNIE BURNS
Pin stripe
◄ The artist makes the paper for her clothes from old cotton garments (see PAPERMAKING), frequently using the fibres of an identical piece of clothing. At its most basic, the technique is to pulp the fibres, then to lay the pulp over an actual garment in between two boards. A car is driven over the boards time and again to impress the pulp to the shape of the garment. Alternatively, a vacuum-formed mould is made from the garment and the pulp is applied to that. Another piece by the same artist is shown on the right.
61×51cm (24×20in)

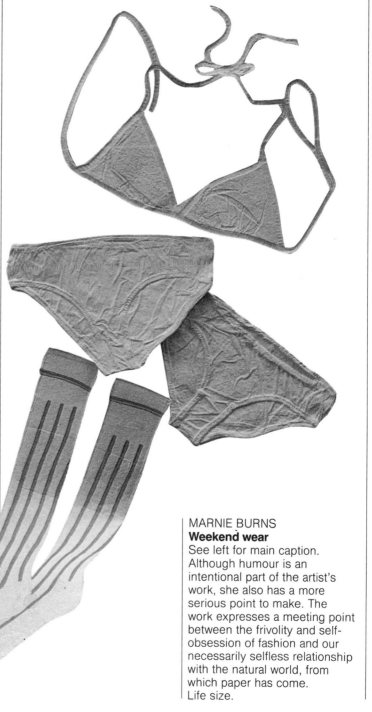

MARNIE BURNS
Weekend wear
See left for main caption. Although humour is an intentional part of the artist's work, she also has a more serious point to make. The work expresses a meeting point between the frivolity and self-obsession of fashion and our necessarily selfless relationship with the natural world, from which paper has come.
Life size.

MIKE CHASE
Horny little devil
The title is a deliberate pun to help the wearer assume the correct character during performance – this is not a decorative or carnival mask, but one devised specifically for use in the theatre. It is made using the PAPIER MÂCHÉ layering technique. A clay head is first sculpted, from which a negative plaster cast is made. The papier mâché is layered into the cast, allowing an extra layer at the edge for strength, then painted with acrylic. Finally, an elasticated strap is attached across the back.
Life size

LOUISE VERGETTE
The dance of the moon through the sky
The piece is a fine example of how paper can be used as a substitute for traditional sculpture materials, such as wood or cast metals. A rigid wooden armature is made first, and covered in chicken wire to create roughly the shape of the finished piece. The mesh is then covered with PAPER PULP, building up the surface as if with clay. When dry, the pulp is painted with a variety of water-based paints. The mirror is made from fragments of coloured glass stuck onto a wooden backing and grouted. Inspiration for the piece came from a symbolism personal to the artist.
110×70cm (45×28in)

LIZ TARR
Bust with crown
◄ Technically and emotionally similar to the large sculpture on the facing page, the two sculptures here are built up with PAPER PULP over a wire armature. To create a smoother surface, tissue paper is layered over the pulp. Quilted fabric and a lead heart complete this piece.
Height: 53cm (21in)

LIZ TARR
Harpy
The pedestal is constructed from wood, plaster and wire to give weight, but the figure is made in a similar way to the piece on the left. Both sculptures are varnished. The images have evolved from the artist's interest in the creatures that inhabit the human subconscious.
Height: 47cm (19in)

DEBORAH SCHNEEBELI-MORRELL
Sun God
◀ Made in a similar way to the piece right, the theme of this piece derives from the myth of Apollo, the Sun God, whose lover was turned into a sunflower. The figure here holds a sunflower aloft, symbolizing desire. Once again, the piece is made with confidence and simplicity.
63×43cm (25×17in)

DEBORAH SCHNEEBELI-MORRELL
The treasury of all desire
▶ In this complex piece, the frame is made from cardboard covered in layers of PAPIER-MÂCHÉ, and the figures, urn and motifs from papier mâché layered over Plasticine moulds, then cut away and re-assembled. Once the complete structure has been assembled, it is painted with acrylic and sealed with matt varnish. The artist describes the motifs as loosely symbolic of human growth and potential. The title is borrowed from a Tibetan Buddhist chalice seen in a museum. The "naive" style, pure colour and timelessness of the piece are reminiscent of traditional folk art imagery, which the artist admires.
79×79cm (31×31in)

ANNABELLE CURTIS
Relaxing
Originally made as a
commission, the tree trunks are
disproportionately wide
because the image was
intended to be cropped through
them. The artist has made
skilled use of coloured papers
and traditional PAPER SCULPTURE
techniques to create a gently
humorous image.
30×45×7cm (12×18×2½in)

DEBORAH SCHNEEBELI-
MORRELL
Three-part invention
▶ This poetic PAPIER MÂCHÉ
sculpture is made by layering
newspaper over a Plasticine
mould, which is cut away and
re-assembled. The base is
cardboard. Symbolically, the
three elements are loosely
related: the woman between
the free spirit of the bird and
the strength/virility of the
(male) horse.
Height: 53cm (21in)

DEBORAH SCHNEEBELI-MORRELL
Dolls
The dolls are all made using the traditional PAPIER MÂCHÉ layering technique, layering the paper over Plasticine moulds. Lengths of elastic are threaded through at the shoulders and hips, pulled taut and the ends knotted, so that the limbs can move and the dolls be made to stand or sit. Gesso is applied to the surface of the final layer of papier mâché, then painted with acrylic and finally sealed with matt varnish. The design of the doll was influenced by a papier mâché doll from Mexico, owned by the artist.
Height of largest: 33cm (13in)

PHILIP COX
The Heavenly Music Corporation
The characters of the figures are beautifully observed and modelled, this time to convey a blacker humour than seen in Philip Cox's other piece, elsewhere in this section. The inspiration for the piece came from a workshop the artist was running in a school, when the children wanted to make gangsters. The artist later made his own version.
Life size

CLIVE STEVENS
Post Office
This piece and the one opposite by the same artist were created as a commission. The subtle use of textured paper – particularly the way in which it is bent at the edge to catch the light or create a shadow – gives a pleasing "papery" yet solid feel to the work. Each piece is cut freehand, then carefully layered to increase the illusion of depth. Much of the success of this piece depends on how it is lit. Thus, this type of PAPER SCULPTURE is not created to be entirely effective in its own right but to work indirectly as a photograph.
50×35cm (20×14in)

CLIVE STEVENS
Scrooge
If the piece opposite evokes
the timelessness of Christmas,
this spirited PAPER SCULPTURE, by
contrast, captures an
expression that is sudden and
fleeting. Note the careful
layering of paper about the face
and eyes, and the delicate
sculpting of the sleeve. Once
again, the lighting is all-
important.
46×42.5cm (18½×17½in)

The work in this section shows the versatility of papercraft techniques in a miniature collection; from the illustrative images of the Woodland scene or the engineering of Lily, to the lyricism of Park and the wit of Root.

The challenge of the natural world as a theme is to represent extremities of scale, from a single flower to a whole vista, so that the papercraft technique and the subject work in alliance. For example, the misty Landscapes are appropriately rendered by layering handmade paper, and the detailed silhouettes of the pop-up shapes in the Woodland scene are necessary to substitute for the absence of surface decoration. In these (and other examples), not only is the medium appropriate to the rendering of the subject, but the rendering is appropriate to the dimensions of the paperwork – a critical factor in the success of any piece.

LYNN CORDELL
Woodland scene
▼ A large and beautifully cut MULTI-PIECE POP-UP, this design uses a variety of techniques. The fence around the tree is a diagonal box, to which the two-piece tree is joined in the form of a cross. The long wall is a horizontal V and attached to it are a sheep and rabbit, which collapse using the trellis principle. The foliage at each side is erected separately by pulling a tab. (Student project: Ravensbourne College of Design and Communication). 80×53×33cm (32×21×13in)

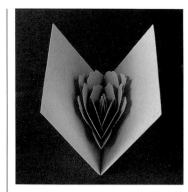

KIEKO NAKAZAWA
Rose
◄ The beauty of this MULTI-PIECE POP-UP flower is achieved not by conventional techniques, but by sewing the pieces through the base sheet, so that the finished construction is both neater (no tabs) and can pivot more easily. 20×15×4cm (8×6×1½in)

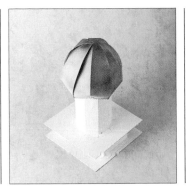

DAMIEN JOHNSTON
Lily
This remarkable example of PAPER ENGINEERING was made as a commission for TV, and shot from directly overhead so that the supporting plates could not be seen. At rest, the lily is closed, but when a plate beneath is depressed, elasticated threads attached to the outer petals pivot them outwards to open. With continued depression, successive layers of petals unfold, layer by layer. When the plate is released, the threads contract and the petals close again in successive layers. Though the network of threads is complex, resembling the ropes that suspend a basket from a balloon, the mechanism operates very smoothly.
Diameter when open: 33cm (13in)

MAUREEN RICHARDSON
Landscapes
These two landscapes are part of a long series of images produced by the artist and sold as greeting cards, being backed onto white card for presentation. They use HANDMADE PAPER, superimposing wet sheets of different colours. The misty effect is similar to that achieved with washes of watercolour, but here the colour is much more intense.
Each 16×12cm (6¼×4¾in)

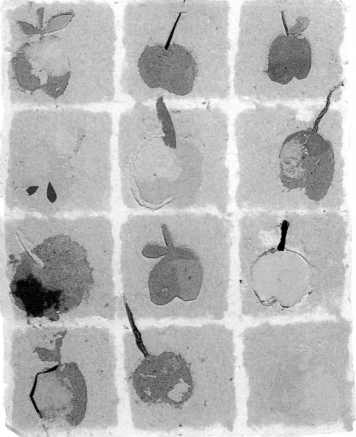

COO GELLER
Tree with apples
The HANDMADE PAPER is made from recycled etching paper, to which onion skins and plant fibres have been added to create flecks of colour. The tree image is an etching print, but other printing techniques have also been used. By making her own paper, the artist is able to achieve greater control over the relationship between the image and its ground than is possible when a print is laid onto a commercially manufactured paper.
53×33cm (21×13in)

COO GELLER
Apples
Using a similar theme to the work on the left by the same artist, this piece is made very differently. It is an example of the PAPER PULP technique, made from recycled etching paper. The pulp is separated into different containers and each dyed a different colour. The image is made by stencilling, overlaying and placing the pulps side by side on a wet pulp ground, then pressing flat.
23×30cm (9×12in)

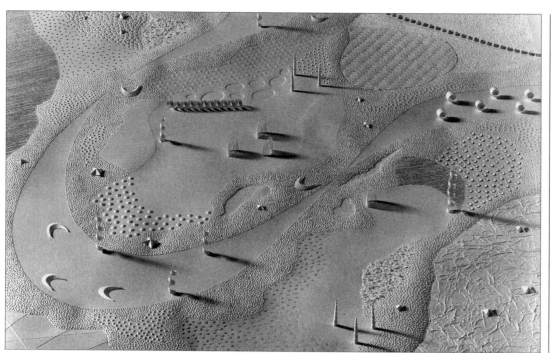

HIDEAKI TOMOOKA
Park
A work of great originality, this playful composition is in contrast to other pieces by the artist. A great variety of techniques is used, including pricking, coiling, indenting, layering, weaving and slicing, to achieve surface textures and low-relief forms that are abstractions of the features of a real park. More than any other piece in the book, it shows the great range of textural possibilities inherent in the surface of a sheet of paper, which are rarely fully exploited.
80×80cm (32×32in)

CONTEMPORARY CHINESE
Bridge across the Yangtse River
Another example of the skill of unnamed Chinese PAPER CUT artists, this design is unusual because it is not traditional, overtly political or cute. The unusual form of the frame adds greatly to the panoramic sweep of the composition. Note also the delicate cutting of the bridge.
18×13cm (7×5in)

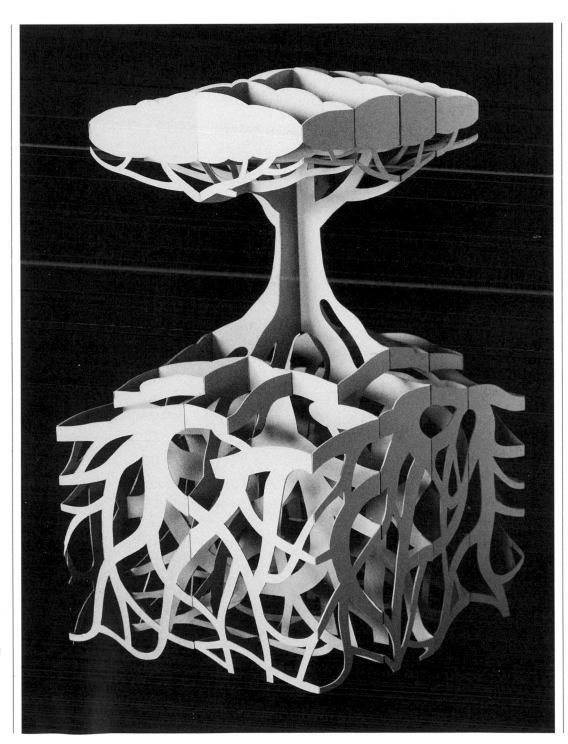

MOTOZO YOSHIZAKI
Root
This piece collapses flat using the collapsible trellis principle. Despite the geometric structure that enables it to flatten, the shapes of the roots are wild and organic, creating a pleasing contrast. Witty reference is made to the size of the roots in relation to the size of the trees above: the piece is apparently upside-down.
26×26×54cm (10×10×21in)

CONSTRUCTED WORLD

This section is the shortest, but could have included pieces from other representational sections, such as Pin stripe, Post Office and Park. Such is the versatility of the work that many pieces cannot, of course, be easily pigeon-holed into a single section.

The constructed world is the ideal subject for model-makers, to whom the representation of a made object offers tremendous scope. So it is refreshing to find the Five implements painted paper cast among the models. Coming as it does almost at the end of the book, it is a final reminder that, although the THEMES sections have presented many paperworks in many techniques, these could never be an entirely representative set: the creative artist will always find a way to surprise us. Some would say that this is the very role of the arts – to surprise and thereby challenge us to examine our preconceptions.

VIC DUPPA-WHYTE
Galleon
Here is an extraordinary MULTI-PIECE POP-UP, designed as a prototype but never used commercially because of its complexity. The artist was a well-known paper engineer, designing some of the better-known pop-up books of recent times, including the classic *Human Body*. The galleon is a superb example of his virtuosity. It is essentially a shaped square-on box, pulled open by two wire hooks, one on each side of the hull. The deck is an example of the layering technique and the rigging is an upturned V. Length: 51cm (20in)

YOSHIHIDE MOMOTANI
Coach

▶ This is a prime example of the technology style of ORIGAMI. It is made from a single rectangle of uncut paper, the ends of which join at the top of the carriage to create the enclosed space below the roof. Of particular interest are the wheels, which are pleasingly circular, and the axles that connect them. The design makes extensive use of techniques that increase and reduce the width of the rectangle, so that it can be narrow for the walls of the carriage yet considerably wider across the wheels.
Length: 11cm (4½in)

ANDREW KEYS
Crane

◀ This design was developed from plans for a real crane and is an example of the MODEL MAKING approach to papercrafts. The problem – as ever – is to interpret the subject in card: to simplify the form where necessary so that the model can be made yet retains enough detail for it to look convincing. Controls at the back of the cab operate the jib and hoist independently, and the cab is able to revolve on the tracks. (Student project: Ravensbourne College of Design and Communication)
48×22×48cm (19×8½×19in)

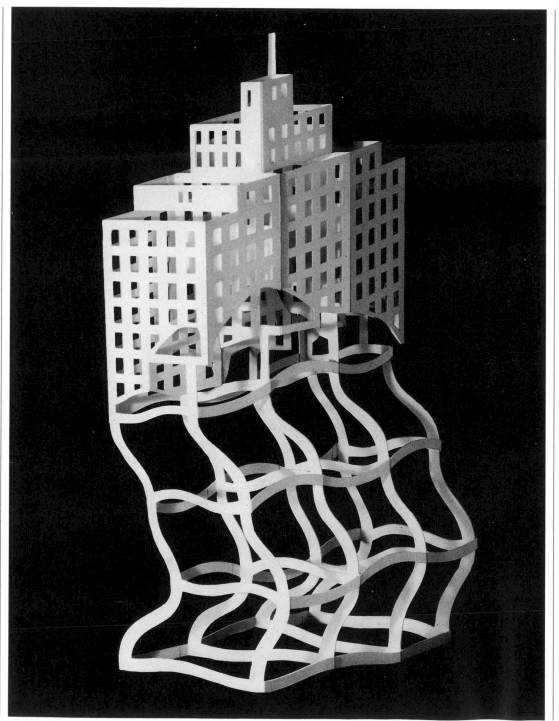

MOTOZO YOSHIZAKI
Drunken building
◀ An example by the artist of the collapsible trellis technique which enables a 3-D design to flatten, this piece has the quirky humour typical of the artist's work. As before, the piece has two levels and the contrast between the two creates much of its visual and conceptual interest.
16×20×45cm (6¹/₂×8×18in)

CAROL FARROW
Five implements
▶ This simple yet distinctive piece uses the PAPER PULP technique, in what the artist describes as the "direct cast method". Cotton linters are pulped, couched and laminated, then semi-dried. The damp paper is laid over the surface of an object – in this instance, a pitchfork – and allowed to dry. As it dries, it moulds itself to the shape of the object beneath. The dried sheet is removed from the object and painted with layers of acrylic wash.
152×152cm (60×60in)

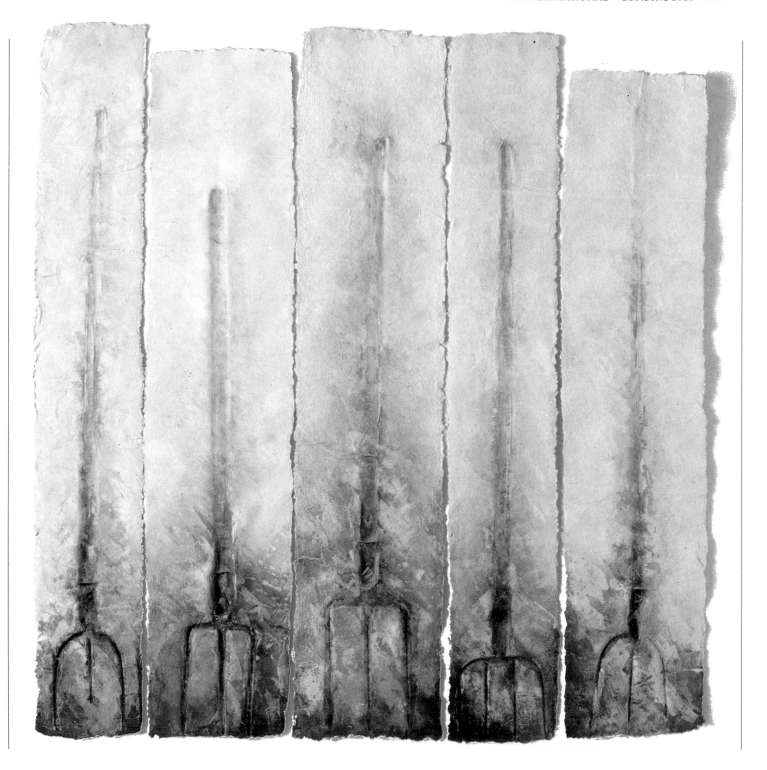

DAVID HAWCOCK
Prehistoric creatures
These playful models are made
using PAPER SCULPTURE
techniques. Note the emphasis
given to the eyes and the use
of curved forms.
Length: approximately 37cm
(15in)

Where the paperworks in the FIGURATIVE section used mainly wet papercraft techniques, the pieces here were made by predominantly dry techniques. This is because the figurative pieces were mostly interpreting human moods and feelings, whereas the creatures here are illustrating likenesses: the artists have been more concerned with form than character, something which the dry techniques are better able to achieve. Though not a characteristic common to all media, this seems to be a current trend in papercrafts, where the dry techniques undoubtedly attract the representational model maker.

With a few exceptions, the pieces in this section were not created because the artist had a deep personal interest in a particular animal. They were made as technical challenges, as commissions, or because they formed part of a larger body of animate and inanimate work. They are mostly ingenious rather than individualistic, logical rather than intuitive.

JUSTINE HOLLANDS
Lobster
The detail and accuracy of the MODEL MAKING on this extraordinary model have to be seen to be appreciated. It is made from a great many pieces, each painstakingly cut, folded and bent to shape. The underside is particularly impressive. As a dramatic bonus, the sections of the abdomen articulate, as do the claws. The outer surface of each piece has been meticulously decorated to create an uncannily naturalistic effect. (Student project: Middlesex Polytechnic) 36×25×8cm (14×10×3in)

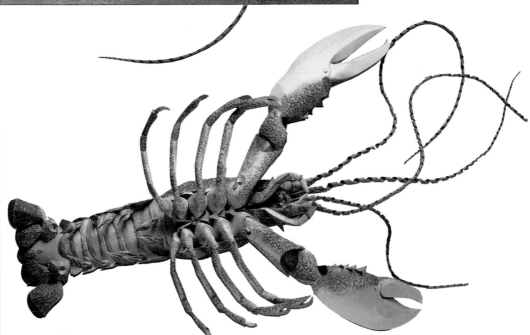

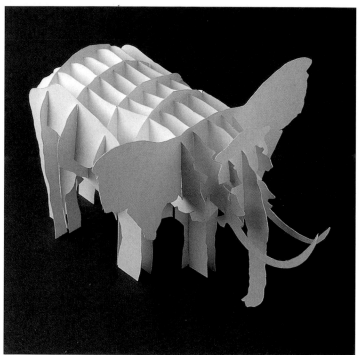

MOTOZO YOSHIZAKI
Elephants
The constructional similarity with the Elephant left is apparent: this design too will fold flat. The artist wishes his work to express wonderment and humour – hence the double tier of elephants and the trunks and tails waving in opposite directions.
21×16×33cm (8½×6½×13in)

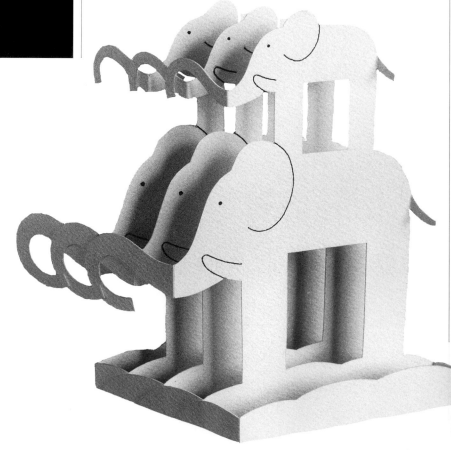

AUBREY SMITH
Elephant
Another example of the collapsible trellis principle, this substantial-looking design will fold flat. Care must be taken during construction to choose cross-sections that coincide with important features, such as the tusks and ears in this example.
Length: 27cm (11in)

DAVID SWINTON
White elephants

This remarkable herd of life-sized elephants was made to draw attention to the plight of elephants in the wild. The sheer scale, apart from being a challenge in itself, succeeded in attracting media publicity for the exhibitions in which the sculpture appeared, and thereby promoted the elephants' cause. A variety of PAPER SCULPTURE techniques are used, but at such an extremity of scale, the main concerns are

strength and durability – the elephants clearly must not wilt and buckle while on show. The legs and body are therefore stuffed with waste paper to increase stability. It takes only two men to lift one of these pieces.

Life size

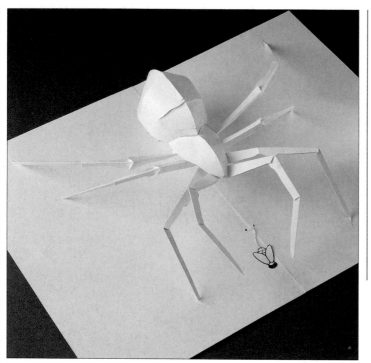

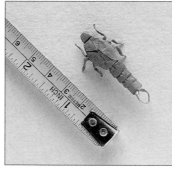

ALFREDO GIUNTA
Insects
▲ ▶ These tiny and beautifully made ORIGAMI models are folded from uncut squares, with the understandable exception of two pairs of antennae, which are cut from the paper, not glued on. As in the Murex shell below, the length and sharpness of the legs are achieved by laminating tissue paper onto metallic foil. Insects with many legs are now common in origami, as technical advances have led to the development of complex bases with numerous free points that can be narrowed and fanned out to form legs, but Giunta makes his designs with uncommon sensitivity for his material and for the form of each insect.
Wingspan of butterfly: 5.5cm (2¼in)

DAMIEN JOHNSTON
Spider
▲ A prototype MULTI-PIECE POP-UP that makes sophisticated use of the upturned V technique. The artist created it to explore the possibility of making realistic organic shapes in a collapsible form. Cotton threads run from the abdomen to the card base to help pull the body into shape as the pop-up is opened. When tugged, the fly causes the front legs of the spider to move as though to entrap it!
Length: 30cm (12in)

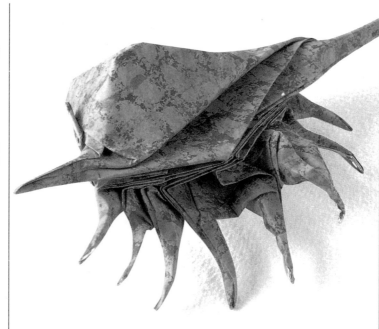

ROBERT LANG
Murex shell
◀ This intricate example of ORIGAMI is folded from an uncut square known as the Bird base, one of the simple abstract shapes from which many designs derive. It is able to hold its spiky shape because the paper is laminated onto metallic foil. Foil does not have the springiness of paper yet is very malleable, so it is able to retain its shape when held in sharp points containing many layers. The hand-marbled paper is not essential to the design, but creates a surface considerably more pleasing than foil.
Length: 14cm (5½in)

DAVID HAWCOCK
Prehistoric creatures

◄ The character of these models – each based closely on a real extinct creature – is achieved by PAPER SCULPTURE techniques and a careful use of coloured papers. Note particularly the similar way in which all the hind legs are constructed and how the differently shaped heads are formed.
Length: approximately 37cm (15in)

THOKI YENN
Animals

► These charming models are made by first folding medium-weight paper in half to form a spine for the animal. An outline is cut with scissors through both layers at remarkable speed, after which the animal is folded into its final shape using simple ORIGAMI techniques, mostly reverse folds. The giraffe is the simplest. It is strengthened with creases down the legs to prevent buckling. Unlike the other models, the cat does not have a crease down its spine. The curved shape of its back is formed by the cut edge of the paper and the "spine" crease runs down the chest and stomach instead.
Height of giraffe: 26cm (10½in)

SUZIE BALAZS
Cat on indian quilt
Compared with some of Suzie
Balazs's other pieces, the
image here is more abstract,
relying for its success as much
on its vivid use of colour and
bold composition as on the
subject matter. The curved,
sleepy cat and the straight-
lined quilt create an effective
contrast. Beads are embedded
into the pulp.
61×50cm (25×20in)

KEVIN PERRY
Goldfish

► Here is a work whose link with paper may not be immediately apparent. The delicacy of the white lines is achieved by a very simple technique. Each line is incised into a sheet of medium-weight paper. The sheet is then placed on a designer's light box (a box containing fluorescent tubes, topped with translucent white perspex to diffuse the light, used by designers to see through several layers of paper, so that an undercopy image can be traced onto the top sheet). The paper to one side of an incision is carefully raised or lowered, so that more or less light can flood through: the greater the separation, the wider the white line appears. Thus, each image can be made to look very different, depending on which edges are moved.
38×28cm (15¹⁄₂×11¹⁄₂in)

ANGELA FREESTONE
Imperial dragon of heaven

▲ This spectacular PAPER SCULPTURE – part low-relief (along the body), part half-round (at the head) – was created as a commission, using white cartridge paper and gold paper laminated over cartridge. The circular scales were meticulously cut to shape and graduated in size along the length of the body to help create a sense of depth. The design is constructed on a complex armature and attached to a base board.
147×103cm (60×42in)

LEE MORSON
Chinese lion

◄ The complex curved shape was achieved by cutting and bending chicken wire, then applying layers of PAPIER MÂCHÉ in the traditional manner. Details such as the toes, teeth and eyes were added later, following which all the chicken wire was removed through the stomach. This not only helped the papier mâché to dry on the inside, but also considerably lightened the structure and so reduced the weight on the left leg. (Student project: School of Art and Design, Swindon College)
Height: 64cm (26in)

JACKIE HATFIELD
Boar

◀ This work is one of a limited edition from the same mould. A clay and plaster model of the animal is made first, from which a multi-piece negative plaster cast is taken. PAPER PULP of a clay-like consistency is put into the mould, then pieced together to make the animal. The surface is painted with gouache, then varnished with a water-based varnish to seal the surface but to avoid the shiny finish associated with oil-based varnishes.
Height: approximately 100cm (40in)

CONTEMPORARY CHINESE
Horse

▲ The PAPER CUTS equivalent of a brush painting, this image is wonderfully spontaneous, yet is made with great precision. Note the careful shaping of the legs, and also how the shapes across the body link distant sections of the design, so strengthening it.
11×8cm (4$\frac{1}{2}$×3$\frac{1}{4}$in)

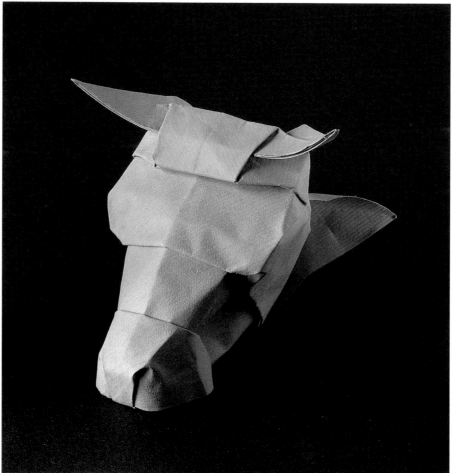

DAVE BRILL
Bull's head
This is an expressive example of an ORIGAMI technique known as "wet folding". The paper (preferably unsized) is dampened on both sides with a cloth or spray before being folded, so that when the design is completed, it dries – or rather, sets – into shape. The advantage over conventional techniques is that the paper can be folded softly and will not spring open, so that origami designs of a pleasing sensitivity can be made. The technique is particularly appropriate for folding animals. However, because the creases are not put in mechanically, the effect can be difficult to achieve.
$19 \times 15 \times 15$cm ($7\frac{1}{2} \times 6 \times 6$in)

AKIRA YOSHIZAWA
Minah bird
A simple and precisely folded ORIGAMI design, this work makes effective use of the two differently coloured surfaces. See opposite for details of the artist and his approach. Dimensions not available.

AKIRA YOSHIZAWA
Sheep
Akira Yoshizawa is acknowledged as the greatest of all paper folders, whose prodigious spirit has inspired and led a worldwide revival of interest in the art of ORIGAMI, starting in the 1930s. He is officially recognized as a Japanese Living Treasure. In his work, he tries to capture the inner character of his subject, rather than attempting a figurative likeness, as is the tendency in the West. For this reason, he dismisses much Origami as "recreational", whereas his creations have "spirit". There can be no denying the exquisiteness of his touch, as seen here in one of his many sheep designs, never before published. The design has been "wet folded" (see opposite) from a single uncut sheet of paper. Dimensions not available.

DAMIEN JOHNSTON
Eagle head
The head is part of a larger piece, commissioned to introduce a series of TV news reports. It was made using PAPER SCULPTURE techniques, particularly curved edges, scored creases and tabs to hold the components together. For all its apparent simplicity, the relatively few curved edges indicate a construction of great sophistication; it would have been easier to make a more complex surface but the resultant loss of clarity may have made it less successful televisually.
Height: 20cm (8in)

DAVE BRILL
Horse
The three ORIGAMI designs on this spread use the wet folding technique. The horse is folded not from a square, but from an uncut equilateral triangle (all the angles are equal), which helps to create the long, slender legs – there is less paper to narrow at the corners of a triangle than at the corners of a square. Unusually for origami, the design has a great feeling of movement.
Length: 22cm (9in)

DAVE BRILL
Rhino
In contrast to the other two pieces on these two pages, the rhino is solid-looking and weighted heavily to the ground. The designer has crumpled and unfolded the paper before folding, to imitate cleverly the wrinkled texture of the skin.
Length: 25cm (10½in)

DAVE BRILL
Giraffe
Like the horse on this spread, the giraffe is also wet folded from an equilateral triangle. Note the attention given to the outline of the design, which creates the poise and grace essential to the character of the animal.
Height: 27cm (11in)

USEFUL ADDRESSES

The following addresses are for papercraft organizations. Each publishes a newsletter, holds meetings or conventions and some sell supplies. They all welcome beginners and members from any country. Please send an s.a.e. for further details.

International Association of Hand Papermakers and Paper Artists

Sophie Dawson
Vanbrugh Castle
Maze Hill London SE10 8XQ
England

Donna Koretsky
57 Rutland Square
Boston MA 02118
USA

Adrienne Rewl
52 Cole Street
Masterton
New Zealand

Origami Artists

British Origami Society
253 Park Lane
Poynton
Stockport
SK12 1RH
England

The Friends of the Origami Center of America
15 West 77th Street
New York
NY 10024
USA

New Zealand Origami Society
79 Dunbar Road
Christchurch 3
New Zealand

Quilling Organization

The Quilling Guild
7 Coniston Road
Morecambe
Lancashire
LA4 5PS
England

The author Paul Jackson, is keen to hear from paper artists and craftspeople, with a view to establishing a central register and putting interested parties in touch with each other.

Please contact him via
55 Tennyson Road, Coventry,
West Midlands.

The publisher and author would like to thank the many artists and craftspeople whose generosity and enthusiasm made this book such a pleasure to compile. We extend particular thanks to those artists who loaned transparencies, and to the following photographers: Robert Grantham (Paul Johnson's "Cupboard"), M. Planchenault (Jean-Claude Correia's folded paperworks), John Wilson for all quilling photographs, Akira Yoshizawa and the Architects' Association (Kisa Kawakami's "Towers"). All the Chinese papercuts were loaned by Florence Temko. The co-operation of Graphic Design lecturers and students at the following colleges was particularly appreciated: Coventry Polytechnic, Middlesex Polytechnic, Ravensbourne College of Design and Communication, Richmond-upon-Thames College and Swindon College. The pyramid and hexagonal elastic-powered "explosives" are copyright designs of Karran Products Ltd., Lightwater, Surrey, GU18 5XQ, England and used by kind permission. For the handmade papers shown on pages 102-103 the author would like to thank Suzie Balazs and Gillian Johnson-Flint.

The author would like personally to thank Kate Kirby at Quarto for her invaluable assistance.

Many thanks also must go to the artists who contributed their knowledge and expertise to the following sections: paper sculpture, Angela Freestone; papier mâché, Deborah Schneebeli-Morrell; pulping, Madeleine Child; papermaking, Suzie Balazs.

p144 Bunch of Flowers: Explosive Pop-Up Cards © – June 1985 to 1995 Second Nature, July 1995 Paper Power
p145 Christmas Tree © 1984 Paper Power
p110 Snowflake Card © 1990 Paper Power